PORTBOU: A CATALAN

MEMOIR

WITH STORIES

FROM WE, WOMEN

Portbou: A Catalan Memoir

with Stories from We, Women

by

MARIA MERCÈ ROCA

Translated by Sonia Alland

Pinyon Publishing
Montrose, CO

Cover Art: Original Plein-air Oil on Canvas of a Rural Landscape
Copyright by © Aleksandra Serova
Dreamstime.com, ID 161974651

Photograph of Maria Mercè Roca by Manel Haro
Photograph of Sonia Alland by Denis Medvedsek

Design by Susan Entsminger

First Edition: July 2020

Pinyon Publishing
23847 V66 Trail, Montrose, CO 81403
www.pinyon-publishing.com

Library of Congress Control Number: 2020940415
ISBN: 978-1-936671-66-3

Acknowledgments

"The Dolphin" appeared in the Fall 2019 issue of *Metamorphoses*.

We thank Rosa dels Vents-Penguin Random House for permission to publish translations of the selected stories.

In memory of Stuart Friebert

~ *poet, translator, and friend* ~

who left us on June 23, 2020

Contents

Portbou: A Catalan Memoir

My father dealt in black market coffee. The packages he brought from Cerbère were kept in the closets among our clothes. The railroad workers came to pick them up at our house. My first sixteen years smell of that strong, delicious odor of roasted coffee, and compared to coffee, everything else has an odor that is pale, without color.

Book One

I'M in tears all day long. No one can get me to stop. Whether I'm in my baby bed or sitting on the toilet, I need to see someone constantly, hear someone that tells me things. My brother, calm and silent, looks at me with his lively, black eyes and from time to time pats me with his little hands: then I cry even more. He occupies himself hour after hour sitting on the floor throwing clothespins into an empty jar, taking them out and throwing them in again. I draw near with an overwhelming need of attention, tug at his hair and pinch him; he complains a bit but puts up with it all. I need you to come home to drive my sadness away and make me laugh.

Summer, in the afternoons, we take our walk. Portbou is a village of stairways: from the tunnel that leads out of the station there are wide, clear flights of steps that tall acacias dapple with sun and shade. All dressed up, my brother and I walk holding my mother's hand without saying a word. She goes down to the village without her wallet, with the house key tied to a hanky because, that way, we won't be continually asking her to buy something. I long for the strips of fried potatoes in thin colored paper bags, decorated with two little coiled antenna. I long to eat the potatoes one by one, with concentration, hurriedly, without giving any to anyone, and then blow up the bag and pop it. I cry as we walk back and forth on the *rambla* because I want potatoes and my mother only has the key and the hanky with a knot in her hands. My mother always says that we won't come down ever again.

If you leave work on time, you come to meet us. What joy to see you approaching from a distance: you hoist me up and sit me on your shoulders and make me laugh. My brother, at a careful distance, looks at us and a relieved smile, of appreciation, is on his lips because you make me happy.

All the laps in the house are mine. I'm always sitting on someone, materially, physically, and the closer I am, the more secure, the better. While I'm there, my brother has no way of claiming a lap; only when I'm finally asleep can he timidly draw near. I continue being the mistress of the laps for a long time. "Papa, can we read this *tebeo*?* You read the vignettes and when you're done you say to me: "Did you like it?" And I always say: "Yes, but I didn't understand it; read it to me again." I want to sit forever on that big, high lap.

We don't have a record player but we already have records. For saints' days and birthdays people give us records and we keep them hoping that one day we'll have a player, and if we're good we can also go to friends' houses to hear them. When we buy it, our player is green and has a handle of grooved plastic. The stories that come out of that disk going around and around aren't

---

* A generic term for a comic, probably one of the popular ones of the time. (N. of T.)

like those you tell me, where sometimes you change things or forget parts. The voice always says the same words, makes the same pauses, has the same music.

PORTBOU is your village and it's on the other side of the world. It's different, artificial, with a very short history. There aren't any peasants, the people don't come home from the fields at the end of the day, as in almost all the other small villages; they don't have animals or a piece of land to grow something. Even though the sea is there, it's not a village of fishermen either, and the church of Portbou is not a small, white maritime hermitage: it's a tall edifice that dominates the village, with a neo-Gothic façade; to go there you have to climb and climb and climb.

Portbou is a village one passes through. Many people who arrive from afar are waiting for the two required years to go by before they can request a transfer to another place. It's a village open to the sea in front and, on all other sides, surrounded by mountains. A new village, with barely any houses that could be called old, or stone-paved streets. Only steps: stairways going up; stairways going down.

Portbou is a village that has distinction. Summer evenings, the people change their clothes and slowly walk up and down from the top of the *rambla* to the pier. Everyone is dressed in his or her best, with elegant shoes. Portbou takes on the air of a small city. In all our photos, we too are spotless, whiter than white, I with patent leather shoes and flared skirt, my brother with a bow tie, impeccable pants, perfectly parted hair; we appear much richer than we are.

The cemetery of Portbou is small and white, and all the dead face the sea. Next to this tidy cemetery, with the orderly dead, are the people who died without receiving the last sacraments and, for that reason, can't enter paradise. One goes there on a narrow path that runs behind the cemetery through a stretch of mountain. There are Protestants, those who have committed suicide, the non-believers, a Communist who was killed, unknown people, foreigners who die in the station, in transit, and whom no one claims: the dead who disturb. Those dead don't face the sea; everything is dirtier, grass reaches halfway up one's leg, quite a few are buried directly in the earth, only a rough cross indicates the presence of a body. Many tombstones don't have names: the dead without identity, belonging to no one. We seldom go there, to this hidden cemetery, and we torment ourselves thinking: "The people who kill themselves, will they go to Hell? And those who don't believe, are they burning in eternal fire?" After walking among these tombs in silence we go to the other cemetery, the white one, the one that faces the sea, the one where the dead deserve to be glorified. We pray before a tombstone without giving it much thought, leave hurriedly, and when we're outside, let off steam with our shouting.

Portbou is full of guards. *Guardia civil*, police, custom officials, railroad workers like you. But full of guards everywhere: they walk in the village in uniform, guns attached at the waist, with their wives and children. In the station, next to our house, there are even more: the place is full of *guardia civil* and of armed police, everyone in green and gray. Some, it's true, with my continually passing by on my way to and from school, know me and greet me, but, in general, they're unapproachable behind the dark glasses they usually wear. I resent them because they impose a language on me that's not mine, the one I speak with you. I never told you but when I go by them I stick my tongue out at them, secretly, and laugh. Still, the guns they always have with them frighten me.

You're from Portbou and are a railroad worker, like your father. You work in Cerbère, in the office of Renfe and cross the frontier each afternoon on the train.* At Renfe payday is the 26th. Each 26th of the month when you come home, you religiously take the pay envelope from your pocket and give it to my mother. She keeps the money. The 26th you both are always happier.

From Cerbère, when it's the season, you bring us sacks of clementines that are transported in train cars. They're little and sweet and fit whole into our mouths. My brother and I swallow them without taking a breath to see who can eat more, and stop only when we start choking.

From time to time, all the Renfe workers are given a military ranking. They issue a card with a rating for each of you, and you were accorded the rank of sergeant; on the back of the card one can read of the honor and duty that each Spaniard has to defend his homeland. You're very prudent and you keep quiet, but I can't imagine your defending anything. They also give you some metal plaques in the form of a rhombus with a large M painted in red that all of you have to put on the lapel of your uniform but, in reality, no one ever wears it. After your death I find the plaque for the last mobilization buried in the back of the kitchen drawer.

---

* Portbou is on the Catalan side of the French-Catalan border and Cerbère is the French village just on the other side, about 5 minutes by train from Portbou. Renfe is the Spanish railroad company. (N. of T.)

LA *Casa Gran** is a building of red stone that is at the entrance to the village, along the road coming in from France. The railroad workers' children play outside under the plane trees in front of its staircase. One hears the children shouting and the wires in front of the building are always full of drying clothes.

You haven't been married very long before they rent you a miniscule attic apartment in the *Casa Gran*. I'm not yet born and you're very young; the attic has a very small entrance door and the ceiling is slanted, and in some spots it's so low that you can't stand up at all.

You love each other there in the *Casa Gran*, in those little attic rooms underneath the roof, and you give me life. You don't know me yet but you love me.

You never speak of it, never hold it against me, but I'm aware of it: no sooner am I born then you have to look for another job; you have the doubtful privilege of being the first in the village with two full time jobs. But I'm also the cause for a change in our

---

* La Casa Gran, literally "The Big House" where many of the railroad workers lived, was the title of this work in Catalan. (N. of T.)

housing, which is a good thing: they grant you an apartment in the train station where the railroad workers who don't live in the *Casa Gran* have lodgings. In the station apartments, the ceilings are high and to go through the door you don't have to stoop.

Portbou's station doesn't resemble the stations or train stops of other villages, all alike, made of stone with red roofs, simply built and welcoming. The Portbou station has a touch of majesty and opulence, and the distribution of the platforms and of the countless rails is impressive, much like a labyrinth; the tracks create a flat and extensive sea, cross and intertwine; the detached train cars move on them without breaks. A grand vault of iron and glass covers the platforms and the Spanish tracks; it's difficult for the light of day to filter through the dome and frightened birds fly from one side to the other; below it there's a gray building for customs, the station's offices, the entrance hall, the bar, and the apartments for the railroad workers. On the other side of the building are the platforms for the French trains and their tracks, which are narrower. The French trains end in Portbou, and the Spanish end in Cerbère.*

One enters the Renfe apartments on the Spanish platform, through the door next to the commissioner's office, right under the station clock. Opposite the mailboxes, before going up the staircase, is the wall for the little prison. People trying to cross the frontier illegally, those who don't have the proper papers, who were found with smuggled goods, are kept for a night before being deported. The wall is made of the thick glass used for skylights; if one sees a light that means that someone is held in there. If it's

---

* Because of the difference in track width the trains could go no further. Merchandise at the time had to be transferred from one train system to the other by hand to continue its transit. (N. of T.)

dark, nothing; if there's a light, I hurry to tell you when you come home.

The staircase is dark and needs painting; dust and paint chips fall on the steps. Sometimes with a sharp point we write things on them and at times we also throw papers from the top of the stairs and spit directly on the ceiling of the little prison.

One of the building's joints permitting expansion is in our apartment, near the kitchen. You're often disturbed when looking at that fissure: you cover it with adhesive tape but with small movements over time, the tape always ends up breaking. In summer thin streams of tar sometime drip slowly to the floor from our seam.

In all the station apartments, the rooms are large, the ceilings very high; in winter, without heating, it's very cold and everyone's comfortable only in the kitchen; we're washed there in a basin and when we're very sick a bed is put in for us. Before we get too big my brother and I put on our pajamas in front of the stove and then make a dash for our bed; we curl up and cover ourselves head to foot. In the winter, we never use the dining room; our life is in the kitchen: it has a square table of Formica where we do our homework, study and play. When we're learning the geography of Spain, we hang a big map of the peninsula on the wall and look for the rivers, the cities, the mountains: names of places that seem to us so very, very far away.

From time to time, especially in summer, my mother shifts the furniture around. The dining room is large and the few things that are there dance about in it, loose, like boxes spread out in a large, empty space: the television on a table with wheels, the dining table with four perfectly set chairs, the buffet with a poorly reflecting mirror, the sofa and the red, plastic armchair that in summer sticks to our thighs. It was the same in the bedrooms: the bed's headboard pushed against the wall, the night table, the armoire at its feet and the dressing table to the right. When I come home from school, when you return from work, everything has been changed: the TV has replaced the sofa, the buffet, the TV; the bed is where the dressing table was, the night table on the other side. Only the square dining table with the four chairs remains in the center. Everything seems different, actually much better; the illusion lasts until we grow accustomed to the new arrangement of the old furniture.

From the house the sound of the trains is loud and clear: the grating of the brakes on the wheels and the brusque jolt of the final movement of the trains upon entering the station, and the short whistle and puffing of those that are leaving. If you're late coming home in the evening, I listen; I sense a train has stopped at the first track and I wait; after a bit I hear you whistling at the top of the stairs: I open the door and burst out running. You're always waiting for me with your arms wide open and you twirl me around.

ONE has a view of the sea from every window in the house. First the canopy over the French platform, then the terraced roofs of the houses, then the sea. With the wind — it's almost always windy — the sea ripples, brimming with white crests. I gazed at the sea for many years but it was years before I saw those brilliant points because for years I had trouble seeing.

I'm sick and you buy me a silver whistle so that I can whistle if I need anything. I'm bored, I hold your present in my hands, and I look at it and whistle; I whistle constantly because I need you to be with me constantly; I have a great need not to be alone. When you arrive from work, you keep me company.

Now I see double. I don't understand what's happening to things. Suddenly they are doubled and the one on the right moves a little and both stay together in the middle, identical, like paper figures that we cut out with scissors to play with. A little blurred but identical, and two. Then I blink many times, rapidly, close my eyes and when I open them usually that thing has become one again. I can't go out by myself because the signs, the houses, the stairs …, everything seems doubled and it confuses me.

To go to the eye doctor in Barcelona we have to catch the first train that leaves Portbou and even if it's summer, it's so early that it's still dark. There are two doors at the clinic, one for the poor and the other for the rich. We enter the door for the poor and inside everything is black because black rests the eyesight and everyone who's there has eyes that hurt. The three of us wait all day, hours and hours and hours, thinking that from one moment to the other they would call us. My hands are sweaty and they leave marks on the black marble of the walls and benches. Once in a while, you and I take a walk and we see Hindus with turbans and silk clothes who are on the side for the rich. During the first visit, the doctor's face is so close to mine that I think: "If I stick out my tongue I can lick his cheek." Meanwhile you're outside and you wait with your hands behind your back, walking back and forth in the hall.

My mother takes me to the doctor: "Doctor, this child has a lot of nervous tics." And the specialist gives us a prescription for blue pills; I have to take six each day: for years and years I go everywhere with those pills. If they drop, they chip as if they were of ceramic; inside the blue coating, it's white. On our way back, on the train platform, she reads the prospectus: "Look, do you see?" she says to me. "Here it promises that these pills will change your character." And she's happy. I don't dare ask what kind of character I have that she optimistically sees the pills changing. You're waiting for us in the station and listen attentively to everything the doctor has said. You don't say a thing: without a word, you look at me, and kiss me. You love me and are unhappy, but I'm sure that you, for one, like my character.

When I finish a container of pills I start another one, and I continue having tics and continue having the same character.

Now, however, each morning I go to a clinic in Figueres,* and in a little room they hang me to straighten my spinal column. They put a sort of leather collar on me that looks like what oxen wear for plowing. A thick cord extends from it to a pulley in the wall. A nurse pulls the cord and ties it very tight and then leaves me alone standing on my toes that barely touch the floor, with this collar pulling at my neck as if my head were about to separate from my body. The leather, so close to my face, is dark and worn, and smells. I keep very still, only moving my eyes, but there's nothing pleasant to look at there. I try to show that I'm calm, that being tied up, hanging, doesn't mortify me. From time to time, I think about things; my imagination carries me very far away. When I ask myself "How much longer?" then time is against me, it has stopped and I think this will never end.

At home, I do exercises for my spine around the dining room table, doing rounds on my hands and knees, first moving one hand forward, then the other; moving one knee forward, then the other. It goes on forever; it's distressing, tedious and boring. I feel like a hunchback and a misfit; I want to be like all the other girls in my class.

---

* Figueres is a middle-sized town about 30 minutes by train from Portbou with more medical services than the village of Portbou. (N. of T.)

17

I'LL never be able to imagine you little, in your mother's arms; to me, you've always been big, tall, well built: you are the one who protects me. I didn't know your father either, or have seen the slightest portrait of him; Grandma is aged, I remember her only as old, dressed in black, supporting herself a little on the furniture as she walked. I do know that, as a young widow, she cleaned offices and rooms accommodating travelers at the station and still preserved the air of a *senyora*. But I only remember her dressed in black, always in black, in eternal mourning. She sings a lot and, with her fingers, beats out the rhythm of some song or other on the table. With the years, her sight has dimmed and she holds objects close to her eyes. Does she see us? My mother makes us visit her each week. "Grandma, it's me." A little after she falls ill, one day, at home, while my mother is cooking, I ask her if she'll die and she says yes, and I'm so upset that a nervous laugh bursts out. But in early August I enter my grandmother's house and you come to greet me in the hallway; you stand in front of me and put your arms around me. Then you kiss me, hug me gently and tell me that Grandma has died. That doesn't bother me much; it's my first experience with death and I don't know what I should feel. But your slow, enveloping embrace moves me. "You can't stay," you say to me, "because Grandma has died." My grandmother had very long, curly hair, gathered in

18

a bun that my aunt did up for her, every other day, in the dining room. She had carried you inside her and had nursed you, and I should have loved her more. You are very tall, very thin, and when you kiss me like that I'm probably too little even to reach up to your chest.

We take the train to Llavaneres, to our other grandparents' house. The first trips last an interminable amount of time; some trains we catch stop at all the stations and stops: we have them memorized and recite them like a lesson. At *Empalme,** we have to get off and wait for the train that goes along the coast: always, absolutely always, we arrive late for the train we'd planned to take. During the trip, so that we don't get bored, we play, read, tell stories. For my brother, you find a seat in Portbou, get him out at *Empalme*, seat him again in the other train, where he doesn't move until we have to get off. I, emerging from the tunnel at Portbou, am already asking: "Papa, do we still have a long way to go?" It's the tedious song that I continue repeating.

I'm entertained if you let me go from my seat to the corridor, holding fast, with unsteady steps, my brother keeping an eye on me so that I don't go too far. When I'm tired of that I make him stretch out in his seat, I open my mother's bag and I comb his hair, make him up and put cologne on him, and to stop me from fidgeting, he puts up with it. When I've half smothered him with the layer of face powder, I begin again: "Papa, when will we get there?" When the train stops or slows down, you stick your head out of the window, look at the station master, at the track switch, and tell us if we have to wait for a faster train or one carrying freight to go by. If we stop for a while and you stand in the space

---

*   *Empalme* (from the verb *empalmar*: to join or connect) is a term referring to a station where train lines connect. (N. of T.)

between the exit doors or go down to the platform, I'm always behind you.

Grandpa controls the track switch. He has magnificent blue eyes, is slender, recites poems. He takes care of the flowers and spreads bread crumbs on the wall next to the house instead of scattering them on the ground so that—he says, seriously—the birds can eat them without having to stoop. At times, he assures us that he doesn't believe in God. Grandma has hair of a white that's immaculate, cheeks of very smooth skin, a full and round body. She has small, dark eyes and laughs a lot.

The grandparents' house is in an uninhabited area, near the main road leading to the town, next to St. Peter's hermitage. They began selling wine there—huge barrels, a damp wine cellar—vegetables, soap, and with the years, the house changed into an eating place: work days they cook for the workers and Sundays for the richer families of Barcelona who come to relax in their vacation homes.

Next to the grandparents' there's the Carmen house, a residence for secular nuns of Saint Gemma Galgani. The door is iron, green, very large, with a peephole that opens when we ring, after we hear the shuffling of approaching feet. We spend many hours there in the summer when there's a lot of work in the bar. It feels like a big dollhouse. It has a garden with magnolias and fruit trees, privets and colorful dahlias; the ground is of gravel and when we run, we raise clouds of dust. At the other end of the garden there's a chicken pen, and a pigeon roost painted in sky blue; the pigeons come and go and from every corner one hears a continuous cooing. We play hide and seek. We sit on the white wooden benches. We look at the pigeons. When it's time to have dinner, Grandma calls us from her own house, through the mulberry trees; we run to the door, open the latch, and go out to the road. "We'll be back tomorrow," we cry. On the outside, trimmed cypresses line the entire length of the garden: we break off the cones and return to our house with full pockets.

In Portbou, for many years there was a plaster head of Saint Gemma that the nuns gave us with its hair gathered in a bun, a very white face and glass eyes. It's fallen on the floor more than once but hasn't ended up broken, only a little nicked. No one in the house especially likes having this bust on the hallway shelves, but a saint is a saint, no one dares to say anything and this sad face lives side by side with us for years and years.

I'm happy in Llavaneres. The mulberry trees from where Grandma yells to us to come to supper were planted by my grandfather; they're big trees, planted close together, the branches mix and intertwine, making a perfect ceiling of leaves. In summer in the shade of the mulberry trees, one is more comfortable than anywhere, and here in Llavaneres it's not like Portbou, where we dress up; here I remember always being in *espardenyes** and a checked pinafore fastened from top to bottom. You help me climb into the mulberry trees, like the boys, one leg here, one leg there, until I sit on a branch and I see you underneath watching to see that I don't fall.

When there's a free table at the bar, I pull you over to it and make you play dominos with me. I like the way you mix them so that all the dominos are hidden under your open hands. They make a noise that is like nothing else but the rubbing of those dominos on the table as you slowly move them around, with a grave look that makes the game very important. We spend a long time, playing

---

* Canvas sandals that are common, casual footwear. (N. of T.)

one game then another, and another, you and I alone, and I never tire of it: you let me win so gently, so discreetly, that I never catch on.

You help load and unload cases from the truck. Usually that exhausts you as you're not used to physical labor and you're tall and thin and don't eat much and are not very robust. You load cases and I make certain that the ones you catch hold of aren't missing a bottle. Afterwards, most of the time you end up wearing a support belt and have to sit down to rest, with a patient gesture that expresses your aches and pains.

I go from here to there accompanying our aunt to buy fish or going with our uncle to deliver cases of drinks with the truck. Climbing up to the driver's cabin of the big green Avia that seems to take up the entire road is quite an adventure. After lunch, with the kitchen put in order, our aunt usually spends hours in the small office ironing. Ironed clothes have a warm odor and I love being there reading or doing summer homework. We listen to radio series: each day a chapter, full of drama, sadness, that wring my heart; at times I find my eyes tearing up.

Some days, in the afternoon, our aunt dresses up, puts on lipstick and a sweet perfume, and we go to Mataró, the closest town, to do errands. When we return Grandma is waiting for us: "How did it go?" And we explain everything to her. At night, with the bar closed, we push the bar stools into the corners, put the chairs on the tables and sweep up. Dust, papers and cigarette butts, filth, everywhere. And when I'm a little bigger, my cousin takes me for the first time to a discotheque and introduces me to his friends. We shut ourselves up in the office where our aunt irons and put on records. "You have to know what's going on," he says to me.

I concentrate as hard as I can but I don't know how to pronounce those foreign names and I never learn to do it.

For a long time, I see one year ending and another beginning here in Llavaneres, on your watch, on your big, round, gold Festina. When the hand arrives on the twelve the number thirty-one disappears and a one, all alone, appears in the little square: it's the New Year. A quarter of an hour before, so I won't miss it, anchored to the watch you have on, I look at the moving hand. It seems very important to me that one year is ending and that another is beginning; it's very exciting. "Today is the day for the man with noses, yesterday was for the one with ears."* We pass Christmas and New Year's here in Llavaneres, with the grandparents, uncles and aunts, cousins; every year the table is very long, holds a lot of people, and I remember always being at your side. All of you drink a lot — the empty bottles accumulate on the floor, in a corner — we eat a lot; we laugh, talk a lot and very loudly. Hours and hours we sit together at the table; the joy for us is that we're together. No one is in a hurry; life is there around the table. We play "the wooden shoes of God," pounding hard with our glasses on the tablecloth. I look at you; you're with me and I'm happy. I like the pink champagne: I dunk the little rolled pastries and the glass is full of crumbs.

---

* A joke played on children, for everyone's amusement, the last two days of the year where on the 31st they're fooled into looking for a man with as many noses as days in the year and, on the 30th, for the man who has two ears for each month of the year.

AND you deal in contraband. When the church bells ring the angelus, you stop work; sometimes, returning from school, I see you coming up and we go home together. We have lunch right away; you catch the one o'clock train and, without a break, you start your second full-time job in Cerbère. And you deal in contraband. You take liqueurs to Cerbère; coffee to Portbou. Every other day you carry a kilo of coffee in your hand and another one or two hidden in your trousers, at your waist, with the uppermost button undone and the belt tight.

The kilo packages that you bring from Cerbère are wrapped in French newspapers: there are four small quarter-kilo packs in each package. The small packs are shiny and smooth and are illustrated with pictures of a naked black woman and a lion.

Our closets have the odor of coffee because the packages you bring are mixed in with our clothes. I see you as if you were here: in the kitchen, you have just arrived in the evening and without taking off your jacket you undo your belt, roll up your shirt and pull out the two kilo packages you're wearing over your undershirt. I catch them, press my face to them and take in their odor; I fill my nostrils with that smell I love.

The railroad workers come to the house to pick up the coffee. Some are regulars and when I open the door and see them, before they say anything, I know that they're coming for the coffee. But on occasion I see a person I've never seen before and I'm afraid it's someone who wants to trick us: that it's a trap and that you'll be denounced and taken away. I don't know where, but that you'll be taken away. When I'm alone in the house and I hear a knock on the door, I'm always afraid it's someone who has come for coffee and I never know if I should say we do or we don't have some. But nothing ever happens and for years and years you continue carrying coffee inside your trousers, with the coat of your Renfe uniform draped over your shoulders.

I want to know exactly how much you earn for each kilo of coffee that you carry. "One *duro*,"* you say and I think that it's not worth it for so little: so much work to buy coffee in Cerbère, hide it under your jacket, go by Customs as if nothing was wrong, knowing that you're doing something prohibited and, after arriving home, take it out, readjust your belt and keep the packages in the closet, waiting for the railroad workers who ordered them to come and pick them up. What you do, smuggling coffee and liqueurs, is the contraband for the poor.

We buy cognac and anise liqueur on credit and we pay when you've collected the money in Cerbère. The man who sells it to me in the store always spreads a page of newspaper on the counter and places the bottle on its side at the top; he makes it roll, wrapping it in the paper and stops it at the other side of the counter, just as it is about to fall: the bottle makes a sound rolling over the wood that's solid and special. Sometimes someone owes us money and my mother says we're not selling him any more

---

* A duro was worth about 5 pesetas, equivalent, at the time, to approximately 10 cents on the dollar. (N. of T.)

coffee: in the end, though, she always finishes by giving it to him and telling you that it's the last time.

There's a man who comes to the house very often: at times he comes for the coffee and at times he comes just to be here. He lives alone. He comes and plays with me and gives me little, black, French candies wrapped in transparent paper. They have a very strong taste and stick to my teeth. I don't like them very much but don't dare refuse them. His pockets are always full of them. This man makes me sad because he doesn't have anyone, and for me, not to have a family to come home to in the evening is a terrible thing. But he also troubles me with his watery eyes and his odor that neither you nor the other men I know well have. When he's transferred and comes to say goodbye, he kisses me and I put up with this strange odor in silence. He fills my hands with those candies. Later you tell us he died and I think that if he didn't have anyone, no one must have gone to his funeral. For many years when I open drawers I find the candies he gave me that I hid so that I wouldn't have to eat them.

Like the other railroad workers, we can buy at the *economat*. It comes once a month; one never knows the exact day, but there are rumors, the news goes around, and when it arrives all of us are prepared. The *economat* is a train, and the individual cars are the shops. It's installed in a kind of hangar, a huge, dark structure, the floor full of grease, traces of machines that had been kept there. It has the odor of a closed in space and one's eyes get lost looking into its far corners; you can't make anything out. The cars of the *economat* are set on the tracks: the car where the railroad workers sleep, the shop-cars, the stock-cars and the coal-cars. They're made of wood and when I walk in them the floor creaks. They are lit by one sad bulb hanging on a wire from the ceiling; everything is in semi-darkness.

The articles are arranged against the walls, on shelves, as in a sort of rudimentary supermarket. We always buy very hard, very salty, dried cod. And cans of peaches in syrup, and pineapple. And cases of oil. Bleach. Bars of soap. Sugar. Rice. Chocolate. Lots of candles, because in Portbou often the lights go out. Champagne. For Christmas, we buy *torrons*.* And tomatoes in glass containers, and chickpeas, and lentils; everything much cheaper than in the stores.

The official, at the entrance of the car, notes the articles and quantities we're taking in his notebook: he wears a dark blue smock and when he finishes writing, he puts the pencil behind his ear. We leave the car loaded, set the bags in a corner of the platform and go to get the coal. With a shovel, the person in charge digs into the mountain of coke that takes up the entire car and fills our sack with its shiny balls. You come to pick us up and carry the bigger packages. Afterwards, we put what we've bought in our storage room and in the tall, narrow cupboard in the kitchen that serves as a pantry. The coal has a lot of beetles and at night they run around the kitchen and the cat plays with them; each morning we find some dead on the floor.

---

* A kind of nougat made of crushed almonds and honey. (N. of T.)

I GROW up with the conviction that the guardian angel is with me and that if I'm its friend, nothing can happen. God is constantly looking at me from on high. He's a god that protects the just and helps the poor. I pray before going to sleep and when we travel and the train is about to pull out, all four of us cross ourselves.

You never go to Mass. Many times, however, my mother makes you go: "Let's all go to Mass," she says. And you quietly resign yourself to it; the Mass seems longer to you than to me. I look at you: you kneel down and get up a little out of time, always later than the others. You don't know the prayers, never take Communion; it's clear as day how seldom you attend. I encourage you inside myself: "It's almost finished, Papa, we're about to go out." Afterwards, outside, everything returns to normal, and I'm happy again: my mother is pleased because you've gone to Mass and you're at peace because you've made her happy.

Saturdays, I play on the terrace. It occupies the entire top of the station and is wide, so long that it never seems to end. Each of the railroad workers' families has a shed with a sink, the washing machine, some useless piece of furniture, and other kinds of junk. I have toy kitchenware that the carpenter has made for me, a big kitchen with checked curtains like the ones we have at home, with little shelves: a kitchen just like a real one. There are wires for hanging laundry inside and out, and with the wind the clothes dry in no time. You can see everything from the terrace: the mountains and the main road, the cemetery, the village, the sea, the church.

Inside our shed, my dark-haired friend with the thick braids and I make an altar. Placing one case on another and covering it with an old sheet, we make an altar for a Virgin we found in the house, gold colored, with flaking paint and turning black. We put the Virgin in between two glasses, one on each side, with a few flowers, and play at being two sisters, almost nuns, who live together in that little house, and who are extraordinarily good. We're also poor. We're called Maria, both of us, because we can't find another name that seems as saintly to us. We make lunch with cut up grass and hang our clothes out and each time we pass in front of the altar, we bend our knee, and if we pass too fast and do it badly, it's because we don't have enough faith. We speak to each other with the formal "you": we talk about the weather and about helping people who are poorer than we are; we say short prayers. We keep playing this way until, suddenly, we stop being such good friends. I don't know why. Then I take down the altar and hide the Virgin in a drawer.

But on Sunday, I still go to Mass. I leave Mass, go down the street from the church, cross the square with the pine tree, look in the carpenter's windows and see the piles of sawdust and take in their odor, pass in front of the fountain with the small figures, enter the tunnel to the station, go through the hall where they sell tickets and exit onto the platform. I look at the trains, stationary, on the tracks, the people, the *guardies civils*, and I look at the time on the clock that's just beneath the door to the stairway of my house. I'm in a hurry, always in a hurry, always anxious to arrive home, as if, outside, I don't feel well, and the house is my shelter. And you're waiting for me. We go out together to take a walk; we descend once more but now, after the tunnel, we keep going straight, cross the market square, pass in front of the pharmacy and continue down to the *rambla*. If it's nice weather, there are always people walking up and down, and children in baby carriages. Everyone stops to look at the babies, leans over and pulls the covers down to get a look at them. When we arrive at the *rambla*, I'm already tired of carrying my purse and I ask you to carry it for me and, resigned, you hang it over your arm. Every Sunday you tell me that if I don't need to carry it, it would be better to leave it at home. But you don't scold me, you never scold me, you wouldn't know how. We go down as far as the beach; I climb on the little wall that separates the beach from the sidewalk and I balance myself with my arms extended: if I fall, I lose. Later, you buy me a package of potato chips and I eat them looking at the water. We walk up and down until it's time to have lunch: we gaze at the sea from the pier; at times we walk a little way on the beach. We see my brother who is already going around with a band of boys and girls. I'm elated taking walks with you because I have you all to myself: if you meet someone and spend too much time chatting, my happiness fades a little.

Looking at football games on television bores me, but I'm eager to go with you to see my brother play in the soccer field. It's higher up along the riverbed. The road is stony. If a car goes by, we're blinded by the dust. It's a bare field without a blade of grass. You smoke during the entire game. You never smoke, never carry tobacco but, looking at the game, you light one cigarette after the other, letting them smolder.

A lot of balls fall into the river next to the field, and the game stops, slows down. I honestly think my brother is the handsomest of the team; I want him to win and be the best. I wish it with all my might: I want him to make all the goals and have everyone applaud him. You explain to me that not all the players can make goals, that there are some who have to prevent others from making them. If we lose, we return home downcast.

I seldom go to the movies. Sunday mornings, taking a walk, I always look at the publicity bills for the two theaters that are hung in a tree, but I never let myself be overly swayed by the colors or the photos of the scenes. I like to go to the movies with you because if I don't understand what's happening you patiently explain it to me: it takes me many years before I know who are the good characters and who the bad. Animal films make me suffer terribly, but the cinema isn't an answer to my dreams. There's no actor I idealize, nor do I have a photo of any hung at the foot of my bed. When I go, I buy peanuts from Senyora Claudina: she's like the chestnut seller in stories, with wicker baskets full of good things. The peanuts are roasted, dark and oily: I leave the cinema feeling nauseous but can't resist eating them.

You're a good man. Simple without secrets, affable as is customary with those who have never had anything nor have ever dreamed of having anything. Happy with my mother who, likewise, never had a dowry or an inheritance. Loving with my brother and absolutely loving with me: "The little girl is mine," you say; for you, there's nothing that doesn't include both of us.

I often ask, "Are we poor?" and you laugh about that, and I persist because I want to know how much you make and how much they pay my mother for her work in the store or in the market where she sells or when she machine-embroiders sheets, and I want to know how much books and presents cost. But I have few whims; I never find I'm lacking something. On the other hand, I feel a deep sadness for a girl in my class, slender with dark hair, who when it's time to go out to the playground never has time to play because her mother, instead of a bun with chocolate, puts fish and bread in her bag. The fish has bones and the girl spends half the recreation time with the bun spread open on the wall, picking them out.

"Do you have some money?" my mother always asks when you're at the door ready to leave for work, because you never carry any. Why do you need it if you always go from the office to the house and from the house to the office, if you never enter a bar, if you never buy anything for yourself? My mother handles the money, performs little miracles so that nothing is lacking, and you trust her blindly, completely: "No one would take care of our children like you," you tell her. She makes the decisions and consults you about them, and you approve them always. Everything suits you. My brother and I never hear you argue or raise your voices. You love each other like couples who are poor, for always, in a magnanimous manner that is, indeed, enviable.

One day, when you're in Barcelona, you buy me a Siamese cat. They sell it to you starving, full of fleas, undernourished, with its back legs longer than those in front, with long, sharp nails, and ears disproportionally big. It runs, its body tilted, like the bulls when they enter the square, climbs up the curtains, climbs up our legs, up our backs to our shoulders and there it stays, sitting tight, calm. It looks at everything from on high; the higher the better. I play with it for years and years, and no plaything, no friend brings me more happiness than the hours that I spend with the cat. It gets fat and I grow up, and we still continue playing. When you come back from work, you whistle from the end of the hallway; we open the door and the cat runs out to meet you: you always enter the house with the cat sitting on your shoulder.

Two times a year, in June and in September, trains of pilgrims to Lourdes pass by. The Train of Hope is made of third class cars with stretchers for the sick placed across the seats. When, in the evening, the train arrives on the tracks of the Spanish platform, the *brancardiers** lower everything—the stretchers, the baggage, the wheelchairs with their voluminous and immobile sick—from one hand to the next, through the windows and the doors of the cars, in a precarious and perilous equilibrium, but which is absolutely effective.

The procedure of lowering the pilgrims, passing them to the French platform and putting them up in the other train lasts close to four hours. Many of the village people, especially among the young, go up to the station to help; there's work for everyone. I see you going up and down with the *brancardier* arm band sewed to your shirt, carrying stretchers or with some sick person transported on your shoulders; I take the arm of some of the sick who are capable of walking very slowly on their own or I carry the square cardboard boxes that the Spanish trains prepare and that contain supper. You and I look at each other; we don't say anything but we smile. The station, from one end to the other, is

---

* In French in the text. (N. of T.)

34

full of voices, cries, orders, people who are looking for someone or something, priests, nuns, nurses, *brancardiers* ... The sick press to their chests the bags they're carrying with their personal objects. At the last moment, there's always a sick person left alone on the ground and whom, I don't know why, they take a long time putting on the train.

On the return trip, the pilgrims arrive in the early morning. When they've lowered the sick from the French train, before putting them up in the Spanish one, they arrange them all on the platform and celebrate Mass. All the stretchers are in rows on the ground, the wheelchairs behind ..., the wind carries everything away. As dawn breaks, the sick covered with blankets listen devoutly to the Mass. Perhaps this year, once again, no one was cured, but hope is never lost. For many who look at it from the outside the miracle is there, in this line of sick people who put up stoically with the lashes of the cold wind that persists in blowing at these moments.

YOU know how to read, know how to write. You went to school when you were little. You read old, bulky novels. You are interested in how objects function; you take them apart, but afterwards they never work well at all. When you get angry, you make drafts of letters to the newspapers vigorously protesting all the injustices being committed; then, calmed down, you never send them.

I seldom have to help in the house; I have to study and that's it. If my mother isn't there one day, you and I make fried eggs and potatoes; we don't know how to cook anything else. We cut the potatoes into thick pieces, the width of a finger; the eggs burst open for us, but we like them like that. I study, I don't have to do anything else, not even wash the dishes, or, if only by mistake, pass the dust cloth over the buffet. When I've finished my homework and I know my lesson, I read the jokes at the bottom of pages from *Selections from the Reader's Digest* that you get each month; I always point out that I don't quite understand them, to have you explain them to me and spend time at my side.

In the summer my brother and I come home from the beach famished; we sit at the table and have our lunch. Afterwards, both of us withdraw to our bedrooms and read, and I munch on a crust of bread that I've kept from the meal and feel very peaceful. My hair is wet, the window is open and I'm cold. I have goose bumps but I don't budge. It's a precious moment, everything is silent; my brother is reading too. You've been at work for a while and we only hear the noise of the dishes from the kitchen. While eating my little crust of white bread, I read all the *Patufets* of the second period* that you subscribed me to. I'm ten years old; I read those stories and cry: everyone's so poor, so good, or so bad, but in the end they become good. Everyone has to work so much, little children who have to get up when it's still dark outside. Love stories, old mothers who suffer. I'm always in tears. I read with a knot in my throat; at times I can't bear it any longer and I burst into sobs. My brother laughs at me: "You're crying, what a dope you are." But I like the stories; after reading them, my heart is crushed, hurt, I sigh and think things. I'm sad and reading them gives me gentle pain. I cry and afterwards feel renewed: sad, but strong, in a different way.

To interest me, books have to be sad, I have to suffer reading them, empathize with this suffering, make it my own; I cry for the things that I read but it's my own pain I'm crying about, a pain that, who knows, may be warning us of what afterwards all of us will feel. Everything causes extraordinary emotions in me; the smallest slight in love unsettles me and fills me with anxiety.

---

* *Patufets* are folk tales that feature a small boy, *Patufet*. These are of the "second period" as they'd been popular once before and, once again, were being read. (N. of T.)

YOU send my brother to the seminary for school. He has no desire to be a priest, but that seminary accepts boys like him and provides them with a very economical education. When he leaves, you can't imagine how much I miss him: setting the table for three, not waiting until he comes, not quarrelling with him once he's there ... He comes every two weeks, and the Sundays he stays in Girona, we go to see him. The seminary has extremely high ceilings, frigid hallways, a huge dining room: everything seems cold and out of proportion to me. The bedrooms are small and austere: not the slightest luxury or caprice. The families of the boys that study there, with straightened circumstances, would not be able to have them either. I think my brother is very big; he grew without telling me, without waiting for me: I think that from now on nothing will be the same. When we go to see him, you and my mother look at each other, disconsolate. A week takes an eternal time to go by, but when he comes I don't know what to say to him: knowing hardly anything of his life, of what concerns him, inhibits me. We love each other as always but we've already lost touch with each other.

When he leaves the seminary and comes and goes every day to the high school in Figueres, the distance between my brother and me becomes immeasurable. I admire him, love him as always, without question, like my love for whatever is yours, a love that has been my whole life. But as he grows up, he changes: becomes a little elusive, introverted, little by little participates less in family life. He's like a cold wind; I realize that he doesn't like being with me as much, that he's hardly at home anymore, arrives late for meals, fails his courses. We sit down to eat and he's not there, and my heart cries out to him: "Please hurry," but he arrives late again, you scold him, and the supper, once more, is a little sad.

You think she's pretty, the girl that goes out with my brother. She's tall and blond and walks with an assured air. He never talks about her but all of us know that they've liked each other forever. She's a little taller than I am and seems to me to come from another world, more liberal, more modern; when I see her I feel vaguely anxious: my brother, whom I love, is drawn to a girl who isn't like me. One year we both try out for the "Domund" to collect money for the missionaries. I want her to think I'm fun to be with, and I want to know what she's like, how she says things, how she laughs. I look at her but barely dare speak to her. And my brother, meanwhile, spends hours and hours in his room. He reads, listens to music, studies there; I look at the closed door and would like to go in. Often one of his friends is visiting: what are they doing? what are they talking about? I'm convinced that he doesn't have the slightest interest in me; I feel insecure and unattractive. I don't know if you notice these things. I think: "Perhaps he'd prefer having a different sister," and I feel, with sadness, that his closed door hides a mystery and a world that is separating us.

BOOK TWO

VIOLENCE enters my life abruptly, without pity, and imposes fear, pain; imposes hatred. Harmony is broken: from then on, life at home for all of us seems the same but it's not: everything has changed. I suffer for the first time: a suffering that's shared with the family, but, in reality, it's a solitary thing, because sadness and pain are always personal, absolutely intimate. My sadness, my pain, is intangible and visceral, like a little animal's that doesn't know exactly what's happening, because no one gives me an understandable explanation, because I'm too young to question myself, to dare to question anything. After that, for a time, happy events at home are tarnished, problems weigh more, the days are of a different color. They have hurt you, a special kind of hurt, complicated, unsparing. A hurt that few men have to suffer. A hurt they could have inflicted at almost no other place but Portbou, that strange village, difficult to love and to live in. They hurt your body and your spirit. Overcome by fear, I'm not sure it occurred to me, those first days or later, to tell you I love you.

Documents preserve the memory of what happened: nothing is lost or distorted. I read the legal statements, the certificates of good conduct and the sworn declarations as if it weren't your name inserted there, as if you weren't the man to whom they refer.

It's Saturday; my mother is at Mass and my brother and I are home alone. You return from Cerbère with the passenger train and a kilo of coffee inside your trousers, the belt tight and your coat over your shoulders. It's a little after 7:30 in the evening.

When you step down from the train, the *guardia civil*, who has returned at the same time, asks you and the other railroad workers to accompany him to the customs office. The subsequent declarations from the *guardia* say that he finds you *"suspicious of carrying contraband because of apprehensive behavior during the trip from Cerbère to Port-Bou, suspicions that, furthermore, were augmented by the carrying of something bulky underneath the coat."**

More or less most of your group, who obeyed the guard and wait at customs to be inspected, carry something you all know will be taken from you or that you'll have to pay for. Impatient, upset, you wait together and curse the bad luck for having stumbled upon this new *guardia*, too eager, so overly cautious. But no one comes. You are kept waiting and neither a *guardia civil* nor an inspector appears: little by little, first one then another of your companions leave.

And you leave too. But you can't go out onto the platform and return home because you would have to pass in front of the

---

* In spite of being in a Catalan village, this and all the following statements from the documents were in Castilian, the only officially recognized language under Franco. (N. of T.)

police station and they would see you; so you decide to go down the entire length of the customs room and leave through the hall where they sell tickets. But it's too late.

The *guardia* sees you in that hall and yells for you to stop. Do you hear him? Surely you do, but you don't stop and everything rushes headlong to a crisis. The witnesses' testimonies agree. They saw you *"in the coat, from (your) uniform, walking hastily in the hall towards the exit stairway that, on the right, leads into the village and, on the left, to the Machine Room and other rooms serving Customs."* Furthermore, that *"when (you) started descending the above-mentioned stairway a guardia civil appeared who was running in the same direction."* But the *guardies civils* are never alone: *"Immediately another guardia appeared who in a loud voice told the first one to 'shoot him.' He said this two consecutive times."*

You're very tall, have long legs, and can cover ground easily. After taking the stairs from the hall you go to the left, in the arm of the tunnel that narrows, is poorly lit, and you hurry into the first exit, small flights of stairs with high steps. Once at the top, almost within reach of the building that serves as a dormitory for the steam-boiler personnel, terrified, giving up, you turn around. You stare at the agitated face of the guard who is pursuing you, raise your hands a bit, shrug your shoulders, and ask him:

"What do you want?"

And the young *guardia civil*, without saying anything, pulls his gun from its sheath and shoots at you.

Within a few meters from there, in our dining room, my brother and I are looking at the TV and playing. A little further off, at the church, my mother, in contemplation, attends the Mass.

The shot pierces the air and immediately people arrive at the scene of the detonation. They find the *guardia civil*, pistol in hand, aiming at you and you, standing, wounded, leaning against the wall of the building. The clerk arrives first and wants to help you, but the guard says he'll kill him if he does—life, in such moments, doesn't seem to have much value. "*I helped the wounded man as much as I could, though extremely nervous having heard from the author of the shooting, himself, that I had to leave the man alone and, if I didn't, he'd put two bullets in me ...*"

People began arriving at the house asking for my mother. "She's at Mass," we say and no one gives us an explanation, but the looks of compassion they shower on us intimidate us: something is happening and no one wants to tell us what it is. We wait quietly, feeling small and insecure until friends take charge of us and explain things to us; it's like a film, unreal, difficult to believe. Meanwhile they've gone to get my mother at the church. "There's been an accident," they say to her. But they still haven't taken you away. First one has to contend with the bureaucracy: life doesn't matter; filling out the papers is what counts. The blood that's lost is worth nothing compared to the obligation to immediately inform one's superiors and all the requests that are made to have you taken urgently to the hospital are refused by the military authority, who "*claimed (you) must undergo questioning and sign the document.*"

They take you to the hospital in Girona where you're put into a little room with a grate in front of the door; it's open but there's a guard, day and night, keeping watch. You're under arrest. If my mother wants to go out for a moment to get something hot, a *guardia* follows her. Meanwhile, one person after the other comes to see you: the priests of the seminary, my brother's professors, and the *brancardiers* and nuns of the Train of Hope who come to keep you company. The nun from the hospital looks at you and weighs, on one side, the *guardies* and the grating and, on the other, your bearing and those special visits and concludes that you can't be a bad person; you, however, are kept there as someone who has broken the law.

My brother is still a student at the seminary and goes to see you each day. I'm in Portbou with the friends who took us in. I'm homesick, and don't feel like studying. It seems to me that people in the street look at me and that the girls in the class feel sorry for me. When Father's Day comes, everyone makes something to give to their father, but you're at the hospital in Girona under the watch of the *guardia civil* and I don't know when you'll be coming back. The teacher tells me to make a picture for you that will be laminated; it will be something beautiful for you that you can hang at the head of your bed. I copy Walt Disney's Bambi, that charming deer with long legs and sad eyes, with his head turned and a butterfly, its wings extended, on its tail. The teacher helps me; we paint it with pale colors and it looks like soft cotton. She tells me: "Write that you love him," and I write it in neat letters on one side with the date and my name. The next day they take me to Girona to see you and the night before I can hardly sleep. I'm thinking: "What should I say to you? What will you say to me?" On my way there, with the picture inside its envelope in my hand, I have anxious doubts: "Will I be able to hold my pipi? Will I keep from feeling nauseous?" Those days seem endless, but even when you're back in Portbou, nothing is like it was before.

After the hospital, at home, you stay in bed for a number of days. The wound heals well but we're waiting for a trial. I wonder: "What will they do to you? Will they take you away?" I'm very unhappy. *Guardies civils* come to our house. One of them tries to be friendly and hauls my bicycle all the way up the stairway.

When they approach me, I have the sensation of falling into a pit; I'm so fearful of them that they don't even make me angry, I don't even stick my tongue out at them in secret. I feel insecure: "What do the village people think of us: do they consider us good people? do they say we got what we deserved?" For so little—that *duro* you earned for each package—so much to suffer. A *guardia civil* asks if we owe money in the stores. "What sort of people are they?" they want to know. "Good people" everyone says; we're too poor, too plain; we hold no mystery or interest for others.

You're sad, it wrings my heart to see you; you don't say anything and look at us with hollow eyes, the eyes of someone who is resigned to leading a sad life.

It's been more than a month since they arrested you and, in the house, in front of us, you never speak about it. There's a pretense of a trial; you and that *guardia* face each other. The events are reconstructed in the office of the station chief. You go in alone; my mother waits for you outside in a small room with two chairs: she sits in one; the *guardia* that shot you sits in the other.

The bullet that entered you at the top of the left thigh lodged next to the sciatic nerve. They didn't take it out for fear that the nerve would be disturbed and that you'd end up crippled. Before piercing the flesh, however, the bullet goes through the handkerchief you carry in your pocket, white, immaculate, perfectly ironed, the one you always have to lend me as I never have one of my own, and makes small holes in the creases of your clothes. The handkerchief is kept in a cellophane wrapper inside the night table and is a mute witness, over the years, of this event. You never want to show me the wound; you don't want to talk about it ever again. You don't have to. The village, full of *guardies*, reminds me of it, every minute of the day. Buried in me, inevitably, there is hatred.

It all ends with five days of house arrest; Renfe grants them as vacation days. They make you stay five days at home as a punishment for disrespecting authority, because that evening, wanting to save the ephemeral profit from the kilo of coffee, you didn't obey the order to stop from the *guardia* or heed the steps following you more and more rapidly in the tunnel. The bullet that was shot at you didn't leave any serious mark on your body, didn't have important consequences. Except in your spirit. The reports deal only with your punishment: no one knows anything about your depression afterwards, about your sleepless nights, your shame, the impotence you feel before the people who take a morbid interest in your situation. Wounds to the spirit are never documented on paper.

They suggest that you request a transfer and leave the village; for a few days, we're enthusiastic about settling in the Maresme,* which is flat with an ample coast on the sea; it's available and not on the other side of the world. I don't say it to you but the first thing I think is that, in any other place, you won't suffer the continual presence of the *guardies*, reminding you, endlessly, of that bad time. I'm sure that in another place, any other place, you will find peace. But you don't want to leave. You're a weak man: you're deluding yourself, you want to live as if nothing had ever happened, as if your spirit, your poor spirit, could heal just like your wound. You're deluding yourself. You'll never forget it: the green and gray colors that pervade the village won't let you.**

---

* A county about 3-4 hours by car, at the time of the event, from Portbou. (N. of T.)

** The colors of the *guardies civils'* uniforms. (N. of T.)

You continue, as always, coming and going between Portbou and Cerbère, carrying coffee in your trousers, because life doesn't stop. From the outside, after some time, everything appears as it was before, but you know it's not so: I imagine how afraid you are, how your heart must throb when a *guardia* goes by you. And so many pass by, and so often.

BUT you're not the only victim that cries and suffers in his flesh in Portbou, this strange, occupied village. Not the first, certainly, nor the last. I'm particularly impressed by that German boy, a student, who was travelling alone and, without realizing it, crossed the Spanish border: he stops at the French customs and shows his documents and can't imagine that a few meters further along there's the Spanish customs and that he has to stop and show his papers again. It's night; he keeps going and as he doesn't respect the signals they find him suspicious, dangerous, and inform the police on the *rambla*. Inside the village, in a bend in the road very close to the beach, they shoot at him unmercifully; he probably doesn't have time to be surprised nor to realize what's happening to him.

They take the boy to the morgue and the car, a Volkswagen that, with all its holes, looks like a colander, they leave in the hangar where the *economat* stops every month. At first, a *guardia* doesn't allow anyone to approach it but when, with the years, the car changes into a pile of rusted metal covered with dust and the bullet holes are perhaps not as apparent, everyone loses interest and acts as if they don't notice it.

Whenever something like this occurs, the village inhabitants listen with horror and shame, are frightened, and shut up. One can't say a word; at home, with everything closed tight, yes, but in the village, no; in the street, in line at the bakery or the fish shop, in the bars, what can one say: everywhere are children, wives, in-laws, friends of members of the police force who find flimsy justifications for the most inhuman and useless acts.

THE summer when I am twelve years old, I start working in a village shop. We sell everything, are very busy and only realize it's nice weather when we have to go outside because a client wants to show us something that's in the window or wants to buy a beach towel or a lantern that we have displayed on the street. There are acacias on both sides of the street and, on the ground, patches of sun and shade make spots that mix together. I go out with the client, listen to him or her, see what the customer wants to buy; afterwards I look up at the sky and then up the street where the stairs mount to the station and our house, and then down the street, towards the promenade along the sea. There are people everywhere, people on vacation, people who aren't doing anything. Outside it feels like a festival day, and I reenter the shop and note the artificial light made by the fluorescents. It's in there that I spend four summers.

I like dealing with the clients, wrapping the purchase, meeting someone I don't know and discovering, first, what language the person speaks, and, afterwards, little by little, how easily or not the shopper can be persuaded, if the decision comes quickly or takes centuries to make, also seeing if the customer shares my tastes ..., all of that has great attraction for me. Most of the time I speak French and am pleased when I'm told I speak it well. I like calculating the price of the purchase in francs, helping the client pay in pesetas, picking out a present. I sell piles of dolls dressed up like girls from Andalusia who have names of flowers, perfumes, cities: names from the South. They're of different sizes, with clothes of different colors, trains of different lengths, but all hold their arms in the air, fingers extended gracefully, eyes shut, with narrow waists, and shoes with high, pointed heels. The foreigners buy the dolls in threes, as presents, and I keep wondering where in France or England, in what houses, all these dolls are distributed, on what piece of furniture they will be eternally dancing. We sell fans with pictures of bulls and towels with scenes of flamenco. And we sell gold jewelry from Toledo and coats of arm with swords made in a series, and plaques of wood with a thermometer and a castanet, and clocks and games and I don't know what else. The shop is always full and we're always on the move: if we're not serving someone, we dust the windows and the display cases; everything is delicate and seems ready to break.

I don't realize that my summers are dreary but I resist starting school again. I want to sleep, be bored, have more time than I know how to fill. In the shop, we have to be constantly attentive, listening to every word, without a lazy moment, without laughing, trying to sell as much as we can, staying on the alert to be sure no one steals anything. Most of the days, getting out of work in the evening, the only thing I want to do is go home: I think about the next day when I'll have to return and spend the whole day inside the shop. I know you think I'm too young to work so many hours, but you don't say anything. As the summer goes by, I feel a growing anxiety.

Some evenings, I leave the shop with my friends; we stroll up and down in front of the tables near the sea front; we buy ice cream, sit on a bench, chat. One year, for the big Saint's Day festival, couples begin to form: one friend takes up with a blond fellow whom I like as well, another with an older boy, whom she marries later …; I end up with a Castilian fellow, very dark, much older than I. He works as a bricklayer, has thick fingers, with hard skin on the palms of his hands, and dark fingernails. I go dancing the first night of the festival and my mother forbids me to see him again.

"My mother won't let me see you anymore," I tell him, very seriously, leaning on one of the stone spheres that are on the *rambla*. For him, already twenty years old, it seems like an entertaining game: he tells me he'll be waiting for me that night at the church. I leave my friends just as the dancing starts, walk along the *rambla*, very dark at that hour, and begin to walk up quickly, skirting the stone wall lining the street. Everything is so dark and silent that, half-way up, I no longer want to keep going; the muffled noise that I hear from the music at the ball urges me to go back. But I can't do it, I can't disappoint that boy — whom I hardly know — who is waiting for me at the church door. When I'm finally all the way up, my legs are shaking and my heart is on fire.

We sit on one of the steps in front of the façade, next to the big door, underneath the saints. I let him kiss my cheeks, my hands and tell me he loves me. I keep still because already, and for some time, it's not been any fun. I tell him, however, collecting myself, that we can't go on like this: I don't know where I've picked up these adult clichés. Before I leave, yet again, he compares my skin with I-don't-know-what fine thing and swears he'll remember me forever. I rush down the empty streets to the promenade: the dancing continues; there are a lot of people, my friends are dancing with their partners. You come by a little later to take me home. I see you and for the first time I have an exciting and confused feeling of keeping something hidden.

I'VE completed my studies in the village and must continue elsewhere, so you put me in a school run by nuns in Girona. I've never left home. Girona seems very far away and, furthermore, I've heard that it's very humid. Months ahead we start preparing the linens: sheets, towels, napkins, blankets, pillow covers ..., everything marked with my initials encircled by little embroidered flowers. We buy the uniform and the smocks: I feel so ugly in that drab, checkered clothing and those striped smocks that I prefer not looking in the mirror.

The first weeks I attend the school, you come to pick me up. The first Friday we pack the suitcase, throw everything in any old way, the bag with dirty clothes packed full; then the suitcase doesn't close. They make us put on the checkered uniform with the white blouse underneath. I'm growing; in a week I've become so thin that the uniform is loose on me and looks as if someone gave it to me. Friday never seems to end, one class after another, lunch, study hour, my afternoon classes, until I hear my name on the loudspeaker and I walk as slowly as I can — "if you run they'll punish you and won't let you leave," I'm thinking — until I reach the porter's lodge.

You wait for me looking at the schoolyard, standing straight with

54

your legs a little apart and your hands behind your back. You hug me, and you do it in a way that all of me fits into the circle of your arms. "Let's go!" I say, though suddenly I don't feel in a hurry, I feel overjoyed leaving the place: an entire week without seeing the street, without anyone there who really loves me and protects me. You carry the suitcase and, at first, we walk fast without saying anything as if we were afraid they'd make us go back. When we've covered a bit of distance we look at each other and begin to laugh. We have a snack, go to the station, catch the train and arrive home. During the trip, I calm down and the homesickness from the week becomes diluted and vague: nothing seems so tragic any more.

Soon I begin to come and go between Portbou and Girona alone; I always have the train schedule on me, I wait at the station, read, I like being alone. When the train arrives, I look for an empty compartment and sit down near the window. Until Figueres, the landscape doesn't interest me; after Figueres, my heart starts beating: the sea appears; then I'm soon at home. It's a voyage full of color, at nighttime, as I usually arrive when it's already dark. The lights in the compartment are yellow and faint, the tunnels aren't differentiated but, in contrast, for me it's full of color. I stand up when we enter the tunnel at Colera, just before Portbou, take down the bag, gather the books and put on my jacket. I'm already there. The train moves in on the first track, passes in front of our house, I check to see if you've come down to wait for me. I walk on the platform quickly, don't see anything or anyone, run up the stairs and, from the end of the hallway, I whistle. The door opens and the cat is the first to come and meet me. I whisk him up and hear him purring, I kiss him, bite his neck gently; he looks at me patiently, doesn't want to be let down: "How many days has it been; you're beautiful!" Then I have to explain everything, one question after another: "What did you do, what did you eat, what exams did you take, what did the nuns say …" My mother asks avidly and you listen; you look at me and listen in silence. Afterwards your lap still waits for me, welcomes me.

The weekends are too short. Saturdays are happy; I go down and look at the village streets, check to see if something is different. I go shopping and end up at the beach; everything is the same. I was homesick the whole week, endured the humid and sticky weather of Girona and, once in Portbou, the wind has blown it all away. The sea is still there, the same; from the pier one sees the bay and the village with the church that stands out and the mountains that enclose it from the other side like an embrace. I walk alone because now I have friends in Girona; I return home, study, listen to records. My mother fixes my clothes, sews on buttons that are missing, washes, irons the smocks with white and green stripes. Sunday, after lunch, a profound sadness overwhelms me. I'm afraid, don't want to leave, don't want to be out of the house for so many days. But you don't save me either; you don't say: "Don't go," and the next morning at six, I catch the train and return to Girona. I see the day dawning through the window. Monday is a sad and difficult day. Tuesday is a day without any pleasure, but Wednesday I already begin to say that the day after tomorrow I'm going home, and, thus, slip away the days, the weeks and the entire year.

"Let me have the pen." You wear it on your suit jacket pocket, with the cap jutting out. I grab it and you grumble but you're incapable of not letting me have it. I love to write with your old black pen; my fingers are always black with ink when I return it to you.

Now we don't dance so much. At times we still do a few waltz or tango steps in the kitchen, and you hold me at the waist and

I bend back and laugh. But now not so often. You've changed, I can see it: I still feel at ease when we're together, and you're the same calm, gentle self, but at times you seem lost, as if you were daydreaming. My mother is your support: she decides, she encourages you to act, to live, but your face has a trace of insecurity and of defeat that now never leaves you. I know what you're thinking, what you remember. I also think of it, but we never say anything.

I FALL in love with a boy who is very tall, very thin, very shy. I've liked him for some time, and I ask my mother to explain what he was like when he was little: she tells me that he was a solitary child. Very good looking, she says, and a little solitary. I feel great tenderness for him: in an album I find a photo of my brother in the Corpus Christi procession dressed for Communion, and his photo is there too, dressed in a sailor's suit, small, serious, and with the same expression that he has now; I tear out the photo from the page and keep it to serve as a bookmark. I begin going out alone Saturday afternoons to try and spot him, and I usually find him on the *rambla* or on the promenade along the sea, seated on a bench, alone or with his friend who's always laughing. It's that friend who calls out and asks me to come join them and starts the conversation because the two of us don't dare say anything to each other. Afterwards, the three of us stroll about for the entire afternoon. We begin seeing each other in that way, from one Saturday to the other, without settling anything, without saying anything. All week long, in Girona, I think of him constantly: "If I don't see him—I think—I won't be able to stand it."

He declares himself in a bar in Figueres: we do it all in a classic manner. It's a small and dim bar, packed with tables and crates. We're sitting facing the wall, side by side, with our backs to the people. "I have to tell you something," he says, and I wait. But he lets the whole afternoon go by, slowly, minute by minute, talking about vague things. Finally, all at once, when there's hardly any hope left, he asks me, in a faint voice and in a hurry: "Listen, do you want to go out with me?" It's almost time for the last train; we run through the dark streets holding hands.

Now we go out together; we no longer have to fake a fortuitous encounter, hide our feelings, always be in doubt, fear the intention and sentiments of the other one, suffer. We're a couple. An intense and full life spreads out before me. Everything is perfect; never have I been so happy.

I'm bored in Girona; I'm more homesick than ever, only live waiting for Friday when I can return home and on Saturday descend to the *rambla* and see him. When we meet it's a magic moment; my heart is bursting; I unwind and am extremely happy. We don't stop talking, don't have enough time to finish telling each other everything. We sit on the terrace of a bar and look at the people going by, or on the pier and gaze at the sea. We give each other books. We love each other. But I no longer go for walks with you: now I take walks with him and if I see you at a distance, I'm embarrassed. I feel I've let you down, that another has taken your place, and that fleeting sentiment sometimes prevents me from being completely at peace.

In the winter we go to a café on the *rambla*, a very old one, with a large billiard table in a corner, white marble tables, and an enormous mirror from one side of the wall to the other, behind the counter. There's hardly ever anyone there. We drink sweet wine with ice cubes; you help me do physics problems and then we talk. It's an intimate, quiet place. Soon it's time to go home and you accompany me to the stairway and at times we still have a moment to sit on the bench near the door to the commissary, underneath the station clock, and say goodbye again.

We talk a lot until we discover that we can also say things with our bodies. If we're lucky and his parents go out, we go to his house and spend the afternoon. We kiss, without tiring, on the mouth, the cheeks, the neck. We read erotic books lying on the sofa; we laugh and take pleasure in reading what we don't dare try out ourselves. We spend the afternoon undressed to the waist: all is sensual, intense, very tender. We smoke, our arms around each other, we read poems, hear the hours ring on the church clock. We're afraid that one day his parents will surprise us, but our apprenticeship is too seductive to stop. "If they come — we say — what do we do?" And we have no idea but we don't get dressed, don't move. I arrive home after having spent the entire afternoon there, nauseous from the smoke and disturbed by desire only half satisfied. You know where I'm coming from and don't say anything, but I sense you are sad and I evade you.

I'm sixteen years old, I wear black bras of transparent lace, and I'm learning with passion the erotic nature of things. My girlfriends don't approve of my wearing those bras; it doesn't seem appropriate for a young girl. No one knows, though, that when we're alone our desire is concentrated on that piece of clothing that makes my breasts appear so white. Disposed, obligated never to consummate our love, we give ourselves over to body play and the emotion we feel is extraordinarily delicate. "Touch me": the supplication is gentle like a prayer.

We write to each other. In the dormitory, the nuns leave the letters on the buffet in the dining room and when we enter, before sitting at the tables, we approach the buffet as if it's of no importance to us, hiding our fear that there's nothing for us. If there's a letter, it's magnificent. His handwriting is small and his letters are short and intense; mine are much longer. "Dearest," I begin, and I explain things. But they're sad letters. I'm longing to go back. "I miss you very much." I'm just as homesick as I was the first year boarding at school; now, however, I don't yearn for home or for your lap. It's his that I miss. "Come see me," I ask him and he comes; skips classes, catches a train and comes to Girona to be with me for a few hours. We go to the Devesa Park or walk up Força Street. We look for dark places to kiss. If we're lucky and he comes in a car, it's fantastic because we can go further, to hidden corners. It grows dark, the windows steam up. Inside it's not cold; we're never cold.

One day when he comes to see me, I skip the afternoon classes. We have lunch, drink a lot of wine. Leaving the restaurant, we take the first road at hand and quit Girona. The weather is beautiful; we go slowly almost without saying a word, thinking that in a short time we will be in each other's arms. We look at the landscape: everything is green and yellow. We come upon a peaceful spot with a little oak tree and a field of alfalfa reaped recently. "Let's stop here." And we stop, spread out a few blankets on the ground and look at the colors of the fields and trees and the clouds that quickly move across the sky. Little by little we start taking off our clothes. "I'll love you forever," we say. The afternoon passes by as quickly as the clouds passing over our heads.

I'm convinced that pleasure is a sin. I'm tormented after having been together, thinking that I have to confess. I don't intend to stop sinning, to not let myself be touched anymore, to not touch him anymore: confession would be useless. I stop taking Communion, only go to Mass when I can't avoid it. The priest knows me too well, is aware of my absences, asks to speak with me in his office. He proposes that I go to confession and I'm not strong enough to object. I leave the confessional unsatisfied. I'm a convinced Christian, deeply mystical, yet, in contrast, I can't live my faith when I'm with him. No one can explain to me that a sin is something else. My body and the pleasure it gives me separate me from you and from God: I continue being of two minds, allowing myself the pleasure, but with a stab of fear and remorse in my heart.

I smoke on the sly and you don't want me to. I sit in a café near the windows and take discreet, quick puffs from his cigarette. But you walk by and see me in the precise moment I'm exhaling the smoke: our eyes meet and I'm deeply pained by the disenchantment I see in yours. In the evening, at home, you punish me. "So you want to smoke?" —you say— "then smoke," and you hand me a pack of black tobacco cigarettes half empty. You sit in front of me and have me light one cigarette after the other. I don't look at you, I'm angry, I'm not accustomed to your speaking to me like that. I go to sleep with a bad taste in my mouth and a cold heart: it seemed to me that you were no longer yourself when you punished me.

IT'S always windy in Portbou. Whole days, whole nights, the north wind blows, howls, frightens us. Afterwards come calm days, a false calm: the wind returns, stronger, more furious. At the beach, one has to weigh down the towel with rocks, put them on clothes: when there's wind, everything takes off, the parasols tumble down, the little children's balls roll away, the mattresses for floating in the water are useless. As much as you stir with your hands and feet, the wind takes you where it will. On the promenade a gust of wind lifts up dresses, makes glasses fall on the café tables. Clothing hung up on terraces dries in minutes; when you hang the last piece, the first are already dry. The wind, during the festival dances, makes the planks of the floorboards move even though they're nailed down; and when the musicians play, the wind carries off the singing and the melodies to some other place. At times, the wind makes the music stands fall down, turns the pages of the pieces too fast; it moves the little paper flags hanging over the dance floor that make a faint rustling the entire night, until they end up breaking. At the height of summer, a year when it's very dry, there are fires and the north wind makes it extraordinarily difficult to control them and put them out: the church bells ring and, because the wind carries smoke and ashes, the village air is not fit to be breathed.

In winter the north wind changes color. It's gray and cold, creates eddies on the street corners, whistles at doors that don't close properly, makes the windows tremble and beds shake. The wind makes gigantic piles of dead leaves around trees with totally bare branches. Everything is clear, the sky without a single cloud, everything purified by the wind. Elderly people can fall if they go around a corner without being on their guard. A violent gust of north wind pushes a train car over and it falls on the tracks like an enormous dead animal. It blows with sudden blasts, stops, blows again. Everyone is tousled with hair blown backwards or forwards, the nape of the neck uncovered, walking fast, shoved by the wind, or huddled against a wall waiting for the gust to die down. If it rains and it's windy, it's no use opening an umbrella because it will be turned inside out and the ribs will be broken. In the cemetery, it blows down the glass pots of chickpeas and beans that, empty and clean, serve to hold flowers at the gravestones: the pots fall, the flowers get mixed and are moved to look pretty at the feet of another dead person. You're from Portbou: you bend over like a tender reed and put up with the wind. If we're walking together on the street, we wait for the gust of wind to pass with our arms around each other.

AFTER the orientation course at the university, disorientated, I stop. I want to earn some money, not have to ask for it at home ever again; I begin to work in Girona in an office. At the end of the month, the cashier calls us up one by one and, with indifference, hands us an envelope with the money; the day we are paid we joke a bit more. I leave the office when it's already night: I see how dark it's getting through the windows; light is fading and the shop signs begin to light up, the car headlights are turned on: it's night. We close the blinds and continue working until it's time to close. Obsessively, everything I write speaks about the passage of time, lost time that never returns. Inside me, I'm always a little sad.

I'm happy talking with him or with my girlfriend who knows me so well. Groups of more than three make me anxious, I'm bored, I feel out of place and uncomfortable. I need to feel that my presence is desired and important, as at home where you always listen to me; I need to be answered, not feel my words fall into a void; I look for intimate, confidential relationships and don't understand nor am interested in anything other than that.

One Sunday, in Portbou, we go to a birthday party. I go unwillingly; inevitably I feel self-conscious there. Chairs are placed all around the room, set against the walls and not a piece of furniture in the middle. I sit down and don't move the entire afternoon: I feel embarrassed and unhappy because he's having a good time and resents my attitude; I drink but don't eat anything because nothing appeals to me. Halfway through the party they put out the lights and bring in a very big box, like the box of a washing machine or a stove; unopened, they put it in the middle and say to the host that it's his present. All of us look and the boy begins nervously to tear open the cardboard and, inside, his girlfriend's curled up and covered with paper, and when she comes out they kiss and everyone applauds. I'm angry with myself because it doesn't please me; I have to pretend that I too find it amusing but in reality I'd like to strangle that girl who came out of the box and who is now dancing, dancing happily in the middle of the room; benevolently I excuse her but, at bottom, I envy her. I keep drinking until finally I have to vomit; they give me coffee and salt and each time I feel worse. He takes me home on a long walk through empty streets, with his friend, the one who always accompanies us, each holding one of my arms. I arrive sad and nauseous; never have I been so depressed. I'm in tears because I'm not capable of enjoying myself, I don't belong anywhere, am comfortable only with a few people, groups scare me and I can't bear anonymity. I need to be loved and recognized, as I am at home, where I'm everything for you.

He says that we're finished, ending our relationship in a "classic" manner. I'm convinced that the desolation I feel will never leave me: "Don't go, don't go …": I cling to him as if my life were departing with him. I cry a great deal, my pain is ample, profound, and in the days that follow I don't understand how things are still in their place and how, without him, I also have to get up, and work, and live.

You don't know anything about this pain of mine because you're already not well. I can't tell you anything about it; I don't know what consolation you would have given me. As normally you never spoke very much, I imagine you would have kissed me and we'd have gone to take a walk together, arm in arm, as before.

YOU'VE become sick. All of a sudden, you change, you're very sad, have no appetite, don't talk. You go to sleep very early, wave goodbye with your hand from the door. You say strange, incoherent things, words that come out wrong. My mother weeps in the kitchen and tells me, in secret, that I should call Girona, call the neurologist who, ultimately, helped me with my nervous tics. I call from the cabin in the station, frightened. The doctor is a man of few words and it's hard for me to explain to him that, we don't know why, but now you are saying strange things, are silent for long periods and that you're profoundly sad.

During the visit, without talking, you persist in showing your left leg to my mother: you want her to explain to the doctor that they shot you there. Seven years have passed since the *guardia* shot you and I'm sure you have not forgotten it even for a day; probably you're thinking that what's happening to you now is related to that episode, and probably it does have a relationship: the suffering from those days has been eating at you all these years and now, finally, has proved stronger than you and has won. This time you don't return home: leaving the consultation, you fall and the doctor has you admitted immediately into a clinic.

They put you into the first available room, a very large room, with a small adjoining room. My mother is crying. Afterwards, during the entire time of your illness, we cry very little. You sleep in that bed that's so high and white; you're very calm. We're all there, but we can't help you.

You have a tumor in your brain. In the Barcelona hospital the visiting hours are set, the corridors and elevators are enormous and cold. They have to operate on you, have to take out the black crab you have inside you and that's eating you and pulling you apart. But first, at six in the morning, as if they were doing it in secret, they shave your entire head without leaving one hair. My poor father, you're totally shorn and silent, because at this point you don't speak; you only look with sad, deep eyes, and I can do no more than squeeze your hand, look at you, give you kisses.

All during the hours of the operation, I keep repeating that if God is with us, everything has to come out all right. If God doesn't abandon you, nothing bad can happen to you. I believe it; I'm convinced that if He wanted it, He would make you well and I ask it of Him with all the persistence of which I'm capable. I'm confident: "If You want him to get well, he will."

A few days after the operation, an afternoon, I'm alone with you in the hospital sitting at your side in a chair. I hold your hand, the hours go by very slowly, the room is dim. Suddenly you seem to come to life again. You look at me: I'm still your beloved little girl. "You're bored," you say with a smile and I hasten to say that I'm not. Afterwards, when I explained what happened, everyone wants to see in that "you're bored," so coherent and well said, a sure sign of recuperation and hope.

The results of the operation show that you won't ever regain the faculties you've lost. You won't talk again, or walk well, or write. But that's all the same to me: you're alive, you look at me, you see me, you squeeze my hands: you're my father, alive. I immediately accept having a disabled father the rest of my life. "We'll take care of you," I think. "We'll take little walks, take in the sun." But the tumor grows inside you rapidly; the doctors give you six months to live. I can go on praying, but now I pray that you won't suffer, that everything happens quickly to avoid your suffering. I pray all the time, but especially so as not to think of anything else, to fill the hours, to make sleep come quickly at night. Praying is the only thing I can do.

I live each day, frightened, with the secret desire to hide, to go away. There's much suffering and perhaps still more cowardice and uncertainty: "Is it true that you're going to die? What is death seen from the outside? Why do you, whom I love dearly, have to die?" But the days gently impel me towards your death. I write a great deal. I copy poems and the words from songs, write letters I don't send. Everything is about death, about thoughts of mourning, sadness weighs on me like an immense rock. I have a vital, urgent need of someone at my side. I speak very little with my brother: the sorrow and the fear each of us feels remain private and solitary.

I MEET a boy from Canada on the train. That day I don't sit in an empty car; he's there, he's attractive and I go in. He's young, has red hair and full lips. He spreads out a map and shows me where he's from and where he's going. We chat the whole trip and become friends. He has to get off at Portbou and change trains to continue on to France, but I ask him to stay the night and leave the next day. It's the month of May and you're at home. After the operation, you're better; you're walking a little, even going down to the platform to take in some sun; you remember some dates, can write your name again.

I ask my mother to let the boy sleep in the empty apartment next to ours. That night we go out, walk about the village, talk a lot in rudimentary French, which isn't his language either. We go over to look at the cinema's posters at the end of the promenade; it's cold, dark, late, no one is around. There, sheltered, in front of the box-office window, standing face to face, the colored photos behind us, we kiss, our mouths come together, one inside the other. He caresses me. I want to believe that I'm happy because I need someone to think about, someone to write to, a face, hands to remember, stories I can tell, a concrete body on which to focus desire. We return to the house late, I show him the apartment where he is to sleep; it resounds with echoes, each room

71

enormous and empty, unwelcoming, with only one that still has a bed and the dressing table. We put on the sheets, the blanket and the bedspread. Once the bed is made, I think of myself staying there, the two of us would be so comfortable and warm. I need someone to be mine, who devotes his time to me, who looks after me. But no: so close to home, you so sick, it's impossible to have such thoughts without castigating myself and being ashamed: "How could I think such things, with my father so sick." And it's not desire I feel: it's that I'm alone and am frightened.

Towards the end of your illness, Grandma dies: her delicate heart can't withstand the sadness of knowing that you are so sick: it is an unexpected death, strange, sooner than anticipated. I go to her funeral thinking that it's a prelude, a rehearsal, for yours, for the real one. My mother wants to bid her goodbye, see her mother for the last time; a friend drives her to Llavaneres. She stays there a while but wipes her tears quickly as you're dying and she can't take too much time.

My brother and I are watching over you at home with a helpful neighbor. You don't say anything, don't hear or see anything. We go into the room, look at you, see that you continue to breathe. I continually ask myself what the moment of death must be like, the precise instant when life departs, the exact line that separates the two worlds. That night I'm impatient only because I don't want you to die before my mother has returned; the hours go by slowly; it seems like an eternal night, without an end.

My brother and I take the train to Llavaneres for the funeral. My brother is solemn: he doesn't say a word, we don't draw near to each other. I confide in him that I don't want to see Grandma dead: I feel I'll never be able to remember you before your sickness, laughing, telling me things; at least I want to retain the image of Grandma sitting at the dining room table, looking at me with those little eyes. But it's not fear or sorrow that's making me suffer even more; there's another sensation eating at me: I'm seventeen years old and I'm alone. I feel profoundly alone. You are dying and no one stronger than me takes me into his arms. I think of that constantly. "If I had someone to hold me and who would let me cry and who loves me and with whom I'd find peace ..." In my distress, I don't know what weighs on me the most.

YOU die the next day. It's June and very hot, a summer that's exaggerated and useless. It's all over. You looked at us and the three of us at your bedside were hoping that your end had come, that you had passed away entirely. It wasn't, however, the most difficult moment; to the contrary, now that it has finally arrived, we have a faint sense of relief. What truly has made us suffer without consolation is your silent and still presence, each day, on the road to this finality; what truly made me cry is seeing you —you, my father, so young, so tall and slender, whom I loved taking walks with, hanging on to your arm, who gave me such pleasure—see you die little by little, see you degenerate, lose your ability to move, lose your strength, your intelligence, your responsiveness ... And even more, see you so sad, finished, beaten, totally dependent on our presence.

The house fills up immediately. I'm not afraid; I go into your room and look at you. You're my dead father, it's all over, I'm not afraid. Everyone is perspiring in the dining room; the women fan themselves. Kisses, hugs, words of condolence. I need something else, someone who is there only for me. My mother, sitting in the armchair, dressed in black, without lipstick, with her hair matted from not being washed for so many days, is the perfect image of the desolate widow.

74

All afternoon, all night, there are people in the house. At times the murmur of the voices grows louder, stops for a moment, then starts up again. The day of your death passes and then comes the afternoon of the burial; today the church bells toll for a death that is one of mine.

We're in a hurry to bury you because it's June and it's very hot. At first, I don't understand why everyone agrees we have to bury you quickly, until someone explains it to me, with much delicacy, because you're dead in there but it's as if you can still understand things: dead flesh, he tells me, falls apart immediately, decomposes and rots; if it's hot, the process is faster; for that reason one has to bury the dead more quickly in summer, for fear of epidemics and because of the smell that they have. When we're at the cemetery, I realize that you too will be looking at the sea.

The next day, the three of us are alone; the sorrow and the yearning truly begin. The cat, from the moment you fell ill, did not enter your room: he waited at the door, in the hall, on top of some shelves. Afterwards, it still takes a long time before he wants to go in: if I grab him by the neck and force him to enter, he struggles to get down and dashes away. He knows you're dead and misses you as well.

IN July the three of us spend a few days in a little village in the nearby county of Garrotxa; friends who also spend their summer vacation there insist that we go and find a place for us in the local hotel. We go there to relax, for a change of atmosphere; we go more to flee the emptiness we feel, after so many months of your illness, now that we no longer have to watch over you.

There's boredom, sadness, and the lack of knowing how to fill the passing hours. I search confusedly for someone, I'm not embarrassed to do it, but there's no one in this village for me. From time to time, we go out with the car, eat in some village, in a restaurant on the road. Sometimes, to entertain us, someone from the hotel we're staying in obligates us, in a friendly manner, to accompany him on excursions to a cold and secluded spring or to a river. These trips, more than boring me, put me into a bad mood; when I'm back and sit on one of the nice, cool benches in the square, I regret not having stayed by myself, alone, to read. I have my 18th birthday during those few days and feel horrified to have reached that age. My brother and I don't talk to each other: now he is the man in the family; he's big, he's distant, someone who knows the things one should think and the sorrows one should have. My mother wears nothing but black and bravely does everything she can to appear lively. I'm sad, unsatisfied, disoriented; completely sad, not for you—the pain I feel for you, my dead father, is still small and will grow only with the passage of time—I'm sad for myself, tired, appalled by this life I have, my life. I don't know what to do, what I should do, what I'm capable of doing. No happiness, no projects, only a thought, repeating, obsessive: I'm alone, I'm alone. I desperately need someone and my anxiety doesn't let me see things, take pleasure in anything, relax.

After vacation, I return to Girona. Girona in the summer is an uncomfortable and hot city; I move about as little as possible each afternoon after work; if I go to Portbou, I'm bored, I feel I can't breathe, you're not there, my mother dresses in nothing but black and my brother works; I don't have friends, I don't know what to do with myself. If I stay in Girona I'm eaten up with remorse for not being at my mother's side. You've been dead for so little time. I come and go; no place is right for me.

From the moment you fall ill, I become more or less passionately taken with the boys I know. I fool myself, I fool them. I don't let them be, writing them excessive letters: at bottom I find them too insensitive, too little interested in my world that requires total and absolute attention, consummate love. They are frightened by my demands and the vehemence of my emotions. I need you; I realize that none of the laps and arms I try out have either the gentleness or the abnegation that yours had.

My mother finds work in Girona and comes to live there. I leave the nuns' residence and we rent a small apartment with low ceilings and thin walls. The furniture of Portbou, so old and bulky, doesn't fit there; the former renters sell us theirs and we find ourselves living in a charming apartment that's modern and very pleasant. My mother and I each bear our pain: she reproaches my lack of tact and company; I'm dying from fatigue and sadness. I'm surly and take advantage of the freedom I have and the little authority held by a complaining woman in mourning.

I dream that you come back after a long time because you're not dead but were in prison. You haven't completed your sentence and I assure you, with fervor, that if for your first leave you follow the rules and return on time they'll let you go home every week. My dream, incomplete, doesn't explain to me why we never went to see you, even once, nor why we thought you were dead, but we're very close the entire time of the dream, and I'm exuberant as if, once again, I've found a great, lost love. I wake up and my heart aches: I can't believe that I won't ever see you again.

Little by little, I realize that it's a burden to return to Portbou. We go now and then for a weekend and stay at our house—so spacious, with such high ceilings. We go to the cemetery, rub the marble gravestone with bleach to keep it white, clean the flowerpots, change the flowers, pray in front of your burial niche. My eyes go through the gravestone, the wall of tiles, the wood coffin and come to where you are and see you. I think about your body that's disintegrating.

I think about your body disintegrating and I think about your heart. I'm convinced of the inexcusable relationship that exists between your death and the pistol shot by the *guardia*. I suspect that you began to die that evening and that you lived a false life for seven years, ending it little by little, undoing yourself little by little. You died that evening, I think, and all the time that you survived was a lie. I know you wouldn't be dead—not so soon, not so quickly—if that *guardia* hadn't shot you. Even today you'd probably be able to kiss me if he hadn't shot you.

I've lost the desire to pray, I no longer pray any more. One precise thing like saving you from death, God did not do. How can I now ask him to deliver me from this strange, painful and vague state in which I find myself? I no longer want either to pray or go to Portbou. My mother is upset: "I can't believe that you don't want to come back." But being there distresses me, I'm afraid there; I arrive in the village and want to return to Girona, to hide. I feel different from everyone and think everyone knows that and is looking at me.

After a time, not living there, my mother must give up the apartment at the station; my brother is in a hotel the short period before his marriage. The decision hardly affects me, I'm barely aware of it, perhaps underneath it all it makes me happy: things happen around me that scarcely touch me. But at the last moment, a few days before giving up the keys, something in me cries out and makes me go there.

I DRIVE to Portbou in the afternoon and stop at the *Punta del Frare*, high up on the ridge overlooking the village, where it's always so windy. From there I look at Portbou and the bay for a long time. The church and the station are close to each other on top, and down below are the small houses, the terraces, the sea. Further along is the white cemetery. I descend the road slowly down to the very bottom, drive through streets without looking at anyone and leave the car near the platform for the French trains. I look at the station building and try to guess which is our kitchen window; it's difficult because they're all alike but I count and I find it: from where I'm at now many times you would whistle and, if we were in the kitchen, we'd open the shutters and watch you come up.

I cross the tracks and go to the platform for the Spanish trains. From there I look at the entire station, the large glass vault that covers the tracks, and I climb up the stairs to the house. There's no light in the little jail. At the top of the stairs, the hallway appears immense, very wide, exaggerated to me, and the light that I see coming in from the terrace and that's filtered by the skylights, I find changed.

There is little furniture in the house; we shared it with others

80

and they'll soon have to pick up the few pieces that remain. The curtains checkered in green that served as doors for the cupboards are still there, as are the brown Formica chairs. Next to the kitchen is the telephone near the buffet that has two drawers and doors lower down; we put the Virgin on it when we'd come once a month. I open the drawer on the right: it's empty; I put my hand all the way in and find dust and crumbs. The dining room is empty, my brother's room also. Mine, in contrast, still has the armoire: I open the three doors and inside, there's nothing.

The last room, yours, is totally bare; there's only the little ball with the bell still hanging from the wall where the head of your bed was that we had installed when you became ill so that you could call us. I open the window and look outside; I look at the sea, at the white crests of the waves that for so many years, without my realizing it, was the water breaking: "I'll never see this room again," I say turning away and my voice resounds against the walls and floor of the barren room.

I'm in a hurry to leave the apartment. I go into all the rooms again, put on all the lights but already some bulbs are missing. Finally I look at the seam, opposite the kitchen, that allows expanding; there you are, standing, as I've seen you so many times when I was little, looking at the crack, moving your head and sighing with resignation.

I go down the hallway, descend the stairway slowly and sit down on a bench on the train platform that's between the door to our house and the commissary's office. In a short time a train arrives on the first track; several people descend. There are still people who know me, who look at me and greet me. When the train quiets down the birds return that had hidden and take up their screeching, going from one side to the other, searching for a tranquil spot to roost among the iron bars of the vault. Pairs of *guardia* calmly walk up and down the platform.

At this point I've seen everything. I slowly cross over to the French side and get into my car. I drive along the road as the sun sinks behind the mountains. I pull up once more to the same place where I stopped when I came. I look at the cemetery and realize that I didn't go there and am happy I didn't: I need you alive, now more than ever. My eyes sweep over the entire village: "My heart no longer belongs here," I think. Before turning my back at the crest of the hills and leaving it all behind, I notice in the movement of the pine branches that the north wind is beginning to blow.

Stories

from We, Women

BOREDOM

MARIA and her mother are in the sewing room: the young girl in a reed chair next to the window. The woman in an armchair in front of the armoire that fills an entire section of the wall. Beside the door, the grandfather clock — that almost reaches the ceiling — was lazily marking the passing time. Between the mother and daughter there's a sturdy table, material, tangible, full of pieces of clothing to iron, and also there's an invisible wall, but even more solid, made of reproach and suspicion.

Whenever Maria looks up from her knitting she meets her mother's eyes, and today, distant and cold, they frighten her. For it's perfectly clear that she's being punished. After lunch, with the clean plates drying upside down next to the sink, her mother took her into the sewing room, did the first row for her, fairly wide, and then ordered her to sit down and not budge from the chair the whole afternoon.

"And pray that your father doesn't find out about it," she said.

For Maria who just turned twelve, the warning about her father doesn't scare her at all, because she's the only girl and her father adores her. She looks a little cross and sighs but begins obediently to work the wool with her small fingers that normally are clumsy enough but that now, full of chilblains that sting her unbearably, move with even less grace. She looks at them and bites her lips to keep the smile inside from showing and, happy, dreamily caresses them, and her heart leaps out the window, flies over the patio, and goes far off, far off …

"Hurry up, it's for today," her mother scolds her, and the young girl reluctantly returns to her needles.

From time to time a stitch escapes her and makes a hole, but it's all the same to her, because what she's doing is useless, long and thin like a sausage, won't serve for anything and is made of remains from rough yarn, reused, of colors that hardly go together, but that's part of the punishment: to keep her occupied doing something not fun or useful and, especially, to keep her closed up in the house. And precisely today, when she's so bored in the sewing room, her brothers are out in the yard; they're playing skittles, just below the window, so she can hear them and want to play with them. That's all the same to me too, she thinks. Maria's brothers, outside of Biel, the youngest, are boys that make off with nests, bathe naked in the pond and chase the girls when they're leaving school. With her eyes fixed on the needles, which are making a little sound that began happy, but is now already tedious — click-click, click-click, click-click — she plays at distinguishing the voices she hears and guessing how many boys there are. Her two older brothers, for sure, and Thomas, the son from the other farmhouse, and the little boy who is complaining because they're not letting him play. She listens a little more, her body tense, wishing with all her might that she could lean over the window. No: Joan isn't there.

Half-past. She passes the yarn over the needles. A row of stitches to the right and one in reverse. It's been a while since her mother closed the window and the boys' voices were harder to hear. Maria looks up and observes her mother: with a serious face, she's darning her little brother's socks using an alabaster darning egg. How angry she is! And how Maria's fingers are stinging! She finishes another row, which includes two holes, and sighs. How boring! Suddenly a spark of hope strikes her: what she's doing, so ugly, could be a piece of blanket to cover new-born kittens, if she can save them like the last time. Maria is thinking things over: when she hid the cat in the attic and no one could find her around the time she was supposed to give birth and everyone thought that she was dead until finally she appeared with her kittens — two black and two blond — that were already more than two months old and no one had the heart to kill them, then yes they did scold her and yelled a lot at her, but after a bit her mother gave her a kiss, told her not to do it again, and that was all. Now, it's different. She won't speak or look at her, as if she had in some way hurt her. And there's no reason for it, the girl thought. Now she's finished the socks and turns the collar of one of her father's shirts that was very worn. Her hands tremble a little, or do they only seem to? But, yes, her mouth is closed tight, not like the other days; so much that it seems she's never smiled, her cheeks are sunken in, she's frowning and her body is strangely taut, as if suddenly she's become old. She can be so gentle when she says to her, laughing: "Maria, Marieta, my girl, what shall we do with you?"

Maria doesn't understand. Not even when she cut her little brother's hair and made an uneven mess of it, her mother didn't get so angry. It's true that when, without meaning to, playing with Joan, they burned the lower field that was ready for reaping, her father slapped her on the back of her neck twice. But afterwards he and her mother covered her with kisses, so anxious at the thought that they could have hurt her … And it was a whole field that burned. To give it a try, she undoes a stitch on purpose and gives the needles to her mother to gather it up. Now she'll smile at me, she thinks and little by little she'll be less angry. But her mother undoes the entire row in silence, and the one before that has the two holes, and returns the needles to her without looking at her. Maria's heart sinks. "What she's done is so terrible?" she asks herself. A little resentment begins to take root inside her. The clock strikes one, and for Maria those chimes have never seemed so sad, so solemn. She raises her head and stares at the mimosa that has turned the color of gold in the past two days. The afternoon goes by as if it wants to stay for an eternity. They hear noises from the kitchen. Maria pours water from a pitcher into a glass with hardly a spill and offers it to her mother.

"Want some water, mother?" she asks winningly, but the woman says no and the girl's heart slowly closes like a shell that, up to then, was open.

All of a sudden, the little boy comes in, his shoes untied, his knees skinned, a slice of bread in his hand and with drops of sweat over his upper lip. He goes straight to his sister, happy at having found her.

"What are you doing?" he asks, grabbing the knit piece with very dirty hands. "You're not coming to play?"

"Your sister is being punished."

His mother's harsh voice surprises him.

He looks at Maria with wide-open eyes. What could his beloved sister have done that was bad, if she's the one who peals his oranges, picks the blackberries that are too high for him, blows on his bites and never rubs his knees too hard, though the dirt that's incrusted doesn't altogether go away? What could his Maria have done? He goes to his mother with a worried face and sits on her lap.

"Why is Maria being punished?" he asks, and looks at her so seriously, so anxious for his sister, that it touches his mother's heart. She shoves his shirt inside his pants and ties his shoes.

"You'll fall," she says. And then hugging him, with a more gentle voice, explains: "Don't worry, Biel: it's big people's business." The boy looks at his mother with his pure, innocent eyes and presses his lips together. He goes to his sister again and rubs his cheeks with the rough wool.

"What's that you're making?" he asks her and Maria whispers in his ear that it's to wrap the baby kittens that have just been born.

The boy remembers perfectly well the uproar that occurred when the cats were hidden in the attic and, with a jolt of fear, instinctively turns to his mother.

"Maria, today you're in for it," the mother says seriously and the boy hurries out of the sewing room in case he's in for it too, but from the door he looks at his sister with devotion and smiles at her.

The afternoon shortens and the rows of stitches grow. Outside, the sparrows chirp. Maria sings a song to herself that the teacher taught them. The last calf that was born cries for its mother. Another stitch lost. Again, Maria asks her mother to fix it and again she only arranges the girl's clumsy work by undoing the row and gives the needles back to her without looking at her or saying a word. Maria's eyes fill with tears of disappointment. What I did was so bad? she wonders. As bad as one of those sins that the priest says blackens the soul and nothing can clean? More sinful than taking wafers from the vestry that day they were hungry? More sinful than freeing the rabbits from their cages the day before the village festival so that they weren't killed? It can't be, she concludes, convinced.

Half-past. The afternoon is ending. The sun that was at first a spot of light on the wall has slowly licked the tiles, warmed Maria's feet for a while and, now, a moment ago, disappeared. On the road, far off, one can hear the bells of the returning cows. The mother lights an oil lamp and the first shadows appear and, with this light, her face is even harder, so hard that Maria is afraid it won't ever be as it was before. The skein of yarn has become so small there's hardly any wool left. Maria stands up, leaves the stocking on the table and goes out of the room under her mother's severe gaze.

"I'm going to pee. I can, can't I?" she asks, insolently.

Outside it's still light. She goes down the kitchen stairs two by two and stands for a moment behind the house. She walks slowly to the end of the patio, with her heart in her mouth. She doesn't hear anything or see anyone.

"Joan!" she cries in a hushed, agitated voice. And the younger son of the owners, tall and lanky, with dark hair and complexion, who doesn't look like the fourteen-year old he's just become, emerges from behind the watering trough.

"I've been waiting for you for a long time," he says to her solemnly.

"They've punished me," she whispers. "Because yesterday someone saw us."

Joan feels his cheeks on fire. Yesterday in the hayloft! The breath of his friend smelled like mint and her eyes were a sea of wheat where one wanted to swim. Their fingers were entwined tightly, until she made a gesture of pain from the chilblains, and he started kissing each sore while she looked at him ashamed and laughing. In thanks, she offered him her lips, so tender, and the boy, damp from sweat, burning as if suddenly his fever had shot up, tasted them. Then he felt a weakness, a sweet dizziness, and couldn't stop kissing the tenant farmer's daughter — with whom four days ago he'd burned the stubble fields, hunted frogs in the pond, and spit on the earth to make mud — who now seemed to him so precious, like a Madonna.

Maria's legs were trembling a little. She stretched out her hands and showed him her fingers.

"They already don't hurt me as much," she says to him, and both of them smile, standing under the fig tree, indifferent to the passing time, only aware of each other, a little afraid.

"Do you want me to kiss you some more tonight?" he asks her, his eyes closed, his voice hoarse.

"If you want," she says.

"Of course I do," he says.

Maria's mother has gone out to look for her and finds her coming back in a hurry, disturbed.

"What were you doing all this time?" she asks her.

"Nothing," says the girl, lowering her head so that she can't see her eyes, that were suddenly shining, "it's that I thought I heard the cat down there. I didn't see her all yesterday and I was worried."

Her mother catches her by the arm and makes her return to the house.

"Go in, you're impossible" she says. "And remember that you're being punished."

In the sewing room, her little brother is fingering the yarn. Maria sits him on her lap and kisses him over and over. She's rehearsing for the evening. The child undoes her braids and laughs, and her heart explodes with a happiness she has never felt before.

JUNE 1975

As it's Saturday, there isn't the usual crowd of boys and girls from the high school who come to the Students Bar during the week to study, go over notes, flirt, or discuss how they'd set the world straight.

Seated at the table in the rear, Lidia is waiting for the boy she likes. She's liked him for three very long months, she likes him a lot and likes all of him: his straight hair combed back, his almond-shaped eyes, the freckles on his face, his wide mouth, his hands, his laugh, his voice, his voice when he says her name — "Liiidia," leaning a little on the first i ... Everything pleases her. Pleases her very much.

They're meeting at the same bar where they go every day, because they don't know any other and because they're so young that they wouldn't dare to go anywhere else. She's done all the assignments she had to do — each one not necessary, almost made-up, hardly urgent — and is waiting for him with a tense body and eager eyes glued to the door to see him the minute he enters. In the square outside, shaded by leafy mulberry trees, one can perceive the high school, which today seems to be asleep.

He arrives right away, in a hurry, frightened that she's not there or has gone without waiting for him. Yes, his friends tell him that it's obvious she likes him, but how can one be entirely sure? He's lit from the back when he enters. Lidia finds him so tall and lithe, so attractive, that her heart begins to throb: he's come and she was so afraid that he wouldn't, or that it would be too late or, still worse, that it wasn't true that he liked her. Her friends tell her that it's obvious he likes her, but how can one be entirely sure? Her timidly raised hand says: "I'm here waiting for you," but he's already seen her, his heart and his eyes found her immediately, because love is a very precise compass that always points to the person loved. He sits opposite her, looks at her and smiles. He thinks she's so pretty and he wants her so much! He explains vaguely what he's been doing, lights a cigarette that they share: audacious, they enjoy putting their lips where the lips of the other have just been; that's, up to now, the most intimate contact they've had. They barely talk. She's waiting. She knows it will be today. Minutes pass, quarters of the hour, then half hours go by. Hardly a word passes between them. He's on the verge, a thousand times, to say something he doesn't say. The light that was entering from the open door grows dim. The clients enter and leave, sit down, have a drink, chat, buy tobacco in the machine: they're alive. In contrast, the two adolescents at the last table form a *nature morte*: they're immobile, tense, suffering from desire that's new and painful. They still don't know what to call it. The afternoon disappears. Soon the last train will be departing.

"Do you want to go out with me?"

Finally. That was it. A few words with little meaning. After hours of waiting. He said them as if they were offspring born from his mouth in a long and difficult birth. Lidia laughs. At last, she thinks, but it took time! And she says, simply, yes, that she'd like to. Then, being practical, she looks at the clock and gathers up the things scattered on the table.

"The train!" she cries.

They walk quickly to the station glancing at each other, laughing like children without knowing exactly why they're laughing: when, without meaning to, they brush arms or hips, it jolts them. I'm going out with him, Lidia thinks, and I don't know exactly what that means. She said yes, he thinks, and neither does he know exactly what the future, from now on, holds for them.

Half-way there, she stops because she has a cramp. She leans against a doorway, puts her hand on her right side and makes a face. "It hurts," she says. He comes closer, very serious, without knowing what to do. It's the first time they're so close and so alone since they've been going out together, for the last six minutes now.

"Is it going away?" he asks, and she tells him that she thinks so.

They come closer and kiss each other, what they've been wanting for so many days. Lips on lips, without moving, only placed, because they don't dare, don't know what else to do. When they think they are suffocating, they stop, separate and laugh; then start again. They're intoxicated with kissing and could stay like this their entire life: outside of kissing, there's nothing and no one. Their heads spin. Between kisses, they sigh.

"The train!"

They run holding hands, fingers intertwined, until they're in sight of the station. They stop and catch their breath. Going out with a boy is this, Lidia is thinking, kissing and running hand in hand. And she says, satisfied, that she thinks she's going to like it very much.

THE DOLPHIN

THEY parked the car in the blue zone, at the entrance to the town; the mother asked the girl to get the ticket. Annoyed, she reluctantly went to the meter, returned to leave the paper clearly visible behind the windshield, and spat the gum she'd been chewing for hours on the ground. Afterwards, mother and daughter went to the Casino where the mother's favorite singer would give an intimate recital in a little more than a half hour, based on poems that he'd put to music in his last CD. Marina doesn't like the singer—though, actually, she's never heard him—she doesn't like poetry—has hardly read any—and what pleases her the least, at this moment, is to go somewhere with her mother. The girl is angry, she's sad, and she's very scared. She's walking like a soul in distress one step behind her mother to tell her without saying it that they don't have to walk side by side, that they don't have to be friends, that they mustn't harbor the illusion that from now on they'll always be together. The mother puts up a brave front, appearing not to realize what's going on.

"I don't know if we'll be cold," she says. "But we were wise to bring jackets because I'm not sure if the recital will be inside or out." Marina doesn't answer, and the mother doesn't insist.

They enter the Casino, a magnificent building from the period of the Indians,* very well restored; as it's still early, there are not many people. It's been decided, finally, that the recital will be on the patio to take advantage of the late afternoon wind that chased away the clouds threatening rain: the organizers thought recitals in the open were always more inviting. They'd put up the stage near the neighbor's garden wall and placed the chairs in a half circle, like a Greek amphitheater. The mother sits in the first row and Marina grumbles because she's embarrassed to be so close to the musicians.

"Look, sweetheart!" the woman smiles tenderly and doesn't give her the option of changing her seat. "In the front row! We can almost touch them."

The girl busies herself with her cell while the people are entering. Suddenly, her mother says to her:

"The song that I prefer is the one about the dolphin that dies on the beach, the poor thing; I hope he sings it. Do you know the one I mean?"

No, she doesn't know it and doesn't want to know it. She doesn't have the slightest idea what dolphin she's talking about, alive or dead. She answers with a vague mutter without looking up from the cell and stays engulfed and protected in her virtual world,

---

* "Indians" refers to the Catalans who returned to Catalonia in the late 19th century after making a fortune in Cuba. They invested in many industries and often built extravagant mansions to exhibit their wealth. The Casino here is probably an example of one. (N. of T.)

until she hears the people applauding: the musicians, with their instruments — guitar, keyboard, violin, miniature guitar with just four strings, accordion, percussion — are already in place. She stores her cell in the pocket of her jeans, puts one leg over the other, and sighs.

With the first pure sound of the chords, the girl looks up as if something has been called to her attention. It's not completely dark yet, but an almost full, straw-yellow moon is rising behind the tousled cypress branches. How strange, she thinks, it's the moon that made me look up, and she can't very well say if she likes it or if it bothers her, but with her eyes full of its light she turns to look at her mother and finds her changed into what could be the statue of a mother, gentle and abandoned, present and absent at the same time, her hands on her empty lap and her eyes glued on the singer. She's aged, she thinks. Perhaps she's gotten older in only a few days? she asks herself. In how many days? She persists: in ten, twelve days? And she well knows that that's the number of days her father has been gone, the days and nights that her mother tries to bear, with as much dignity as she can, being the protagonist of a sordid and typical story of a mature woman who has been abandoned after more than twenty years of marriage, for a woman much younger. Marina's eyes wake her mother up and she slowly emerges from her painful and humiliating universe. She turns, questioningly, to her daughter and smiles, loving as always. That smile touches Marina; she feels contemptible, her heart aches and she asks herself why she's never been able to kiss her or show her, even with no more than a kind word, that she's sorry her father has left. What's prevented her? Once she tried but her consoling gesture stopped halfway. The singer presents the musicians now and the audience applauds enthusiastically. "And the body that your voice caressed," he sings and, as the minutes go by, the girl feels angrier, more disappointed and

101

sad. What is love anyway? she asks herself. Is it worth falling in love, promising to live for the other as her mother did for so many years, if from one day to the next everything can collapse. And leave you like an uprooted tree. What hope can I have, she thinks, what security, who can tell me that now or in a few years the love of my life won't tear my love and life apart as well … No, it's not worth the pain, she concludes. If my father, who is a good man, is capable of making my mother suffer, the person with whom he'd shared a deep love, what won't someone I may pick up on the street be capable of doing? A consoling voice tells her that sometimes there are loves that are like a mirage, eternal and luminous, but she shakes her head: it's a question of chance, she says: love, faithfulness, happiness … everything hangs on a thread. The god of luck moves it as he likes. I'm sure that one day, they'll abandon me like my mother and I'll be converted, like her, into a statue consumed with sorrow.

The singer is explaining to them that the song about the dolphin is a version of a poem by Anite de Tegea, a woman poet from the fourth century BC and that it's about the passage of time and the loss of beauty and youth. "I will no longer thrust my head up from the deep water" — says the dolphin who is young and beautiful and playful — "nor, charmed with my shape, will I show off around the beautiful lips of the ship." And suddenly, hearing this, for the first time the girl fully understands what it means to lose beauty, and that youth fades away never to return. She realizes that her mother is crying silently and feels a deep remorse and, now yes, she clasps her mother's hand that is still held quietly in her lap. They don't say anything, don't look at each other, but don't let go for the rest of the concert. Not even to applaud. It's turned dark and much cooler. By the last song, the moon, luminous, is now high in the sky.

Profusely Illustrated

"Do you want some cookies, sweetheart? I have some very good ones."

Her daughter turns to her and says no. She also says she has to leave right away because Laura has training and she's not sure that she has the house keys to pick up her sport bag. The grandmother wrinkles her brow in concentration and asks:

"How old is Laura now? Twelve?"

For a moment the woman thinks her mother is joking and smiles: suddenly, however, she realizes that she's serious and her heart skips a beat.

"Twelve?" she asks her in a scolding tone. "But what are you saying, Mama! She's seventeen! She'll be eighteen in February."

"You say eighteen? But to me she's little."

"Little. What do you mean?" — she can't get over it — "But Laura's very tall. She's always been tall. I don't understand why you're saying that."

The grandmother quickly changes the subject.

"Are you coming for lunch Sunday? I want to make a roast."

Her daughter nods a yes with her head and gets up from the sofa where she has sat up to now. She hasn't taken off her coat because it's always a little cold in her mother's house. She quietly feels the radiator and notes that it's lukewarm. She asks her if she's not cold and her mother assures her that she isn't, that she's wearing a thick sweater she's fastened up to her neck and, if that's not enough, she puts on a housecoat — "that was yours," she says "the one with flowers from years ago, do you remember?" — and she couldn't feel better. On the bookshelf, over the books, there's a folded paper and, without thinking, the woman picks it up and opens it.

"What's this?"

Her mother begins to laugh.

"It was a surprise, but now that you've discovered it, I can tell you. I've bought an encyclopedia for Laura."

Her daughter, not trusting her ears, makes her repeat what she said.

"What did you say you bought?"

"An encyclopedia. They say that it's really good ..."

"But encyclopedias are useless, now. Let's see, Mama, who sold it to you?" She tries hard to control herself.

"Well, a young man really good-looking. It will be easy. I'll pay each month and when I've finished paying, he'll bring it to the house. We'll see if it can be done by her birthday."

"So how much do you pay each month?"

The woman isn't sure; she looks around and picks an amount:

"600 euros? Yes I think it's 600 euros." Her daughter shakes her head in desperation.

"That can't be, Mama. It's impossible."

"If you say so!" the grandmother sulks. "As you're so clever!"

"But your pension is 800 euros! How can you be willing to pay 600 for a shitty encyclopedia?" she says, exploding in anger.

"Don't get angry. You always get angry, girl; what a bad temper. And it's not shitty. Also, it must be six pesetas. Six euros, I mean. Or sixty. I don't remember. You're making me nervous. It's not your business anyway. It's a present that I want to make her. I don't think I have to give you an explanation!" She changes her tone of voice. — "So will you be coming Sunday? I'll make a roast. And vegetables. You'll enjoy it."

Her daughter nods her head yes again. She has the brochure for the encyclopedia in her hands — a photocopy of poor quality — and is fuming with indignation. Her mother has gone out and returns to the dining room smiling.

"Look what I've found straightening the drawers" — she hands her an envelope: inside, photos from very different times, all mixed together, in complete disorder. There are her parents on their wedding day, very young, in the style of Hollywood actors from the 50's; she and her sister, four or five years old, on Palm Sunday, waving palm leaves; a photo taken from far off where one can see all four, very small, at Montserrat; a photo of the first TV they had; her sister — is it she? — dressed like an angel acting in a Pastoral at the church; and a photo of herself — now there's no doubt it's she — in summer camp in a T-shirt, shorts and a cap. She's a chubby pre-adolescent without any grace. She looks at herself and feels bad.

"How come I was so fat when I was little? You never took me to the doctor's?"

The mother, who was enjoying herself commenting on the photos, looked at her without understanding.

"To the doctor's? But why? You weren't sick."

"But I had a lot of complexes. I was very unhappy, Mama."

"I don't see why. You had your little ways. You were stout. That's true. But you were very pretty. People have different makeups. Like your Aunt Esperanza. Do you remember when she got married?" The young woman shakes her head no. "But certainly you've seen photos of her. She weighed a hundred kilos. I still see her. Her dress pinched her everywhere." She starts to laugh. "And they used to say to her: 'Poor Joseph, be careful that you don't squash him!' Because Uncle Joseph was like a toothpick."

"Mama, I'm going. It's late."

Her daughter is in her room studying; she was going to have her finals soon and the girl is a serious student. She doesn't bother her and goes to the kitchen, opens the refrigerator and closes it again. She has no idea what she can prepare for supper. The most she can do is put sausages on one plate and on another bread and tomatoes, and that already demands a titanic force. She hears her daughter talking on the phone and laughing and hearing her makes her happy. After a moment, her husband arrives, hangs his coat in the entry closet and before coming into the kitchen turns off all the lights she's left on. When he appears, she smiles to herself. Her man is so likeable! In fact, she chose him precisely for that, because he's more likeable than she, because he's more patient, more capable of loving than she is, better at taking care of things. They kiss each other.

"You're cold," she says.

"It's cold," he answers, laughing, and immediately asks, "Where's Laura?"

"She's studying. All afternoon. She didn't go to practice."

Suddenly, the man swears:

"I didn't think to go to the dry cleaner's. I'm sorry. Do you need those pants?" He stops because he notices that his wife is very serious and asks her what's going on.

"They trapped my mother," she says. "They sold her an encyclopedia."

"An encyclopedia?" Her husband starts laughing. "They at least worked hard fooling people …"

"Don't be funny," she scolds him, discouraged.

"Perhaps we can pay for it," he says, and takes the paper his wife reaches over to him, which is only a photocopy in color that announces a *Grand encyclopedia of the world in 8 volumes profusely illustrated.* Underneath, a reproduction on a double page that explains the functioning of a volcano; the names of the different parts are in comic book type labels: the lava, the crater, the chimney … on a child's level, old fashioned and not very attractive. Lower down, the name of the publisher: Mayor Editions. No address, no name, no telephone number. The man shakes his head, leaves the paper on the table and hugs his wife.

"That's a loss. I'm sorry. I don't know where we can make a complaint." He pauses, in doubt, but finally speaks: "Your mother's getting old. Pretty soon she won't be able to live alone. We'll have to start thinking about it."

His wife opens a drawer and closes it mechanically two or three times. Then she leans on the marble and sighs.

"If you knew what I'm thinking …"

"What are you thinking?"

"I can't explain it to you."

"Then don't."

"You'd say that I'm a bad person. Why am I that way?"

"But you're not a bad person."

"Yes, I am."

"Come on, lady, let's drop the subject. I love you a lot. Are you hungry? Do you want us to fix supper? Do you want me to make the omelets? Mine are always delicious."

He hugs her while she cries softly. Her daughter bursts into the kitchen calling for supper and finds her parents in each other's arms, very quiet, as if they were dancing to a very slow song.

GOODBYE

THE faint light that comes in through the blinds is fading and tells her that the end of the afternoon approaches. It's been a long day and an anxious one, like each day she's been living lately. For a while now her husband's been sleeping badly: agitated, breathing hard, perturbed by the painkillers they give him. They both know that his days are numbered; that this afternoon, slipping away, spent together alone in the house, will be one of the last they'll have. They've already spoken about it, casually, without dwelling on it, as one does when speaking about important things in life. No more tears are left to be shed, pardons have been given, the goodbye done, and the immense love they have had their entire life, that they still have, and will have forever, has been said as well. Some months ago, a small armchair was put at the foot of the bed where she has been sitting day and night to keep him company, sometimes with a book in her hands as if she were reading, sometimes with her cell phone, often with a notebook where she lists the things she has to do that now, so overwhelmed by sorrow, she can't remember unless she writes them down. Sitting in the armchair, she's even crocheted a scarf for her grand daughter's doll. From there, week after week, she's seen him becoming smaller. His face has changed. He's much thinner. These illnesses do that. At times, his face was swollen, at times his cheeks were sunken in: his body was changing, a result of the medication and the phases of the sickness that is eating at him, inside, like a voracious worm. She straightens his bedclothes that are hanging a little too much to one side. The daylight is ebbing and now hardly any of it comes in through the blind. Her husband wakes up. "Are you okay?" "Yes." "Do you want to eat something?" "Not yet." Exhausted, he closes his eyes again. She, in silence, begins to undress. She takes off her dress little by little, in an orderly fashion, with her customary modesty, and puts it neatly on the armchair. She walks to the bed making little jumps over the cold tiles. He open his eyes, jolted by the noise of her steps, sees his naked wife and thinks he's dreaming. But he smiles and it seems that the ravages of the pain on his face have softened a little, his nose fills out, his cheeks are less sunken. She pulls back the sheets on her side, gets into bed, covers herself and draws close to the dying body of her man, the love of her life, her support. She'd like to put her head on his shoulder as she used to do before he was sick, but now he's all skin and bones and she's afraid she'll be too heavy. She takes his hand, opens it and places it, flat out, on her pubis, and after a moment, she guides it slowly to her right breast, and then to the left. He sighs deeply, as if the bit of life still in him is being drawn out through his mouth.

"Oh," he says, "Your body! I already feel much better!" and makes a braying-like sound. She's not sure if it's weeping or laughter.

RITUAL

I THINK about my funeral as if I'm looking at a Bergman film; the camera closes in on the saddened faces, eyes full of tears, hands holding on to other hands, the flowers and the initials of my name attached to the coffin. It's a habit that doesn't date from today: for many years, going to one funeral or another, I'd often take my mind off the dead person and begin thinking of how I could improve the ceremony: I thought about the music, the sermon and the testimonials and in my mind graded the priests and most of the time failed them because they said things that were common and empty: spoke about a future life in paradise and didn't say anything personal, authentic, intimate, nothing that couldn't be said at another funeral service, for another deceased. At times I'd leave the funeral very angry, critical not only of the clumsiness of the representative of the Church but of his lack of professionalism. If they worked in a company, I thought, they'd be fired for incompetence. Now I'm not so demanding—now, in fact, I forgive it all and understand it all—but I'm thinking that the day of my own funeral will be the last time my name will be pronounced in public, the last time that those people gathered in the room will think about me, and I'd like—you can call it vanity—that when they leave, they say that the ceremony was moving and a little different. There's nothing more disappointing than to leave a funeral without anything—words, music, tears—having touched you not even for a moment.

So, here we are. You know it's coming to an end. We haven't spoken about it openly, but you know. I'm writing to ask you to take care of organizing my funeral, basically the music and the texts that have to be read, that I've already picked out or at least that you won't have trouble finding. You planned the surprise party for my 50th birthday and you did it very well: it wasn't much of a surprise, but it was a lot of fun. I see I can't ask it of my husband or of my children: I made a try but they don't want to either hear or speak about it and when the hour arrives, they'll be too affected to remember which song or which text I'd like and be capable of finding them. This is the last favor that I ask. And we've done a slew of favors for each other because you and I, we've always loved each other. Our entire life, always together. You're the friend who has shared my suffering but, especially, and much more important, the one who has laughed with me during the happy times. You're my sister. Every day of my life I was grateful to you for what you did when Ignasi had his accident. You took care of the children as if they were yours and neglected your own family to take care of mine. The children loved you so much that I even felt a bit of jealousy. You know that I was always afraid they didn't love me enough. When I was young, jealousy ate me up ...

Today was a good day. I slept pretty well and the pills the doctor gave me are effective. I told him that I needed something that made things seem far away, that helped me keep up my spirit and face the days more or less normally, be able to speak with the people visiting without breaking up seeing their own emotion. Especially I want to be able to be with Ignasi and the boys without feeling the pain that makes my voice tremble and prevents me from having an ordinary conversation. What I need now is to show that nothing's going on. I'm happy because I even have enough strength to dress myself in the morning and I don't weep so much. We all know what's happening. We've had our moments of raw truth, of goodbyes; we've forgiven each other everything without saying as much. It's all settled. Now, it's not hard for me to forgive: let's say that it's all somewhat the same to me, that nothing has much importance. From the day they diagnosed my sickness, I've asked myself if I've done the right things. It's hard to generalize. What things? The ones when I was young, a little less young, older? I've arrived at the conclusion that I've lived without being fully aware. That the years have passed with a sigh, without my ever thinking that time was scarce, that it was going to end. As everyone does, I suppose … If I could go back in time, I'd be with the children more and work less. It was their father who raised them and he did it very well. Let me translate: a job that ruined me. Hours and hours for a miserable income and no security. If I were to live my life again, I'd be a functionary. All my life working for my own account and putting up with it to enjoy a pension and now the result is that I won't collect it. Bad luck. I don't want to get upset over it.

But it's obvious that my moods don't last. I'm not always so serene. From one moment to the other, my feelings can change.

It's been like going down a slope slowly: no sooner do I realize I'm going down then I see behind me that I'm very far down and that it's impossible to climb back up. Now it's okay. It seems easy to say, but accepting it's coming to an end has been a sickness more serious than the illness itself. There are still times when my mind deceives me and I think: what if it were possible to reverse everything? And if there were a miracle? — ah, the angels! And that idea hurt me a great deal. Afterwards, it was hard for me to accept reality again. The mind can go on vacation, but the body that's closing down makes me keep my feet to the ground: when I go to the bathroom, I don't put on the light so that I don't have to look at myself. I don't know who I am. I look terrible and I'm sorry about that because, seeing me, no one can doubt I'm dying. On the other hand, I have hardly any pain; the medication helps me, but I sleep a lot. That amazes me: I'm seated on the sofa, it's five o'clock, I look at my watch again and it's five thirty. I've slept a little. At night, I look at the alarm clock and it's three. I look at it again and it's four thirty. I go jumping from one hour to the other, as if they were stones in a river, now one foot, now another; I propel myself into the night and, sooner or later, the day returns. Each day brings the light and each night has an ending. That's very important to me because I'm not so afraid of the day; there are more things to distract me, and distractions help me not to think and to pass the day. Ignasi and I are fine together, we act as if nothing is happening: we look at films or the iPad or the cell — it's a bottomless well of foolishness that entertains me for a while — or I make lists for things he should buy for supper. We don't plan further than tomorrow or the day after. We do it naturally, as if I were recuperating from a serious sickness, but a temporary one. Still, from time to time, I have periods of anxiety that I wouldn't know how to define, a mixture of shortness of breath, of restlessness, of profound discomfort; I open my mouth searching for air that can't find its way into my lungs, I want to cry and my voice doesn't sound, I'm dripping with sweat. In those moments, dying paralyzes me with fear. Other times, it's as if I see myself from afar, split into two. I think: that woman is dying. And the woman is me. There are moments when I need to be alone and others where being alone terrorizes me and I, like a little dog, search for company. I speak little because I have hardly anything to say. I've already taken leave of everyone in the house.

Now, the ceremony. I'd like it to be religious, not because my faith can move mountains, but because when I was young, Christian faith and culture occupied a large part of my life. Also, secular ceremonies at funeral parlors are poorly done. They've tried but haven't succeeded in giving them either personality or force: they're stiff, the script always the same, and of a childish sweetness. They recount a story that's a metaphor of life and death — it must be, otherwise — that tells of a train where people ascend and descend from the cars ... And another story that talks about a desert island and its gifts and its meaning ... And it's all read with practiced solemnity. Everything's done not to frighten, not to really talk about what has gathered so many live people: a dead person. The texts of the Gospels, in contrast, are powerful, serious, disturbing, apocalyptic ... There, for sure, everything truly ends and without remedy ... It's always impressed me when they say: "Go out to receive him, angels of the Lord ..." Yes, angels please me. They're benevolent and kind, but also brandish spears; they have wings of silk but at times look with very severe eyes. Some years ago, I used to write letters to them. I burned them all a few months ago, because I'd have been very ashamed if they were found and read. Do you see? That's one of the things that upsets me the most: to think that someone — even if it's Ignasi or the boys — will empty my drawers, the closets, the shelves of the study ... What's most intimate, uncovered, my weaknesses, my sentimentalities ... I was very sentimental when young, and emotional, and I've lived little setbacks as if they were authentic tragedies ... And, instead, now that everything is the truth, I'm completely self-contained. To make some headway, I've taken advantage of periods when I feel better to clean out my drawers and shelves. It's tiresome. It's unbelievable the foolish things that can be found in the night table, things that for me have a meaning and a significance, a story behind them, and that I love a great deal, but what for other people—even for my sons—are nothing more than objects, and at times very run-down. I threw away many things but tons still remain. The picture of the mountains that you like so much is for you. And if there's some clothing that you'd be happy to have—the reversible leather jacket that I lent you occasionally and that became you beautifully—or some handkerchief, or the mustard colored top with the high neck that's new ... In other words, whatever you wish, you choose. Luckily I don't own any property and my inheritors won't have to quarrel. Ignasi will live in the apartment as long as he can; afterwards the boys will have to divide it between them: they'll manage; my two sons have always had a complicated relationship ... But my things ... I look up from the paper and I see clutter everywhere ... Yes, most certainly I've kept too much: papers, pictures, books, notebooks, music, posters ... Let them do what they want with everything ... I threw away the diaries I wrote when I was young—for almost ten years. I read them and didn't recognize myself in them. As for the pictures, after looking at them so much over the years, I no longer see them, I don't even know whether I like them, I only know they're there and that some of them have accompanied me all my life. To empty an apartment is always to experience a small death.

I'm telling you about the letters to the angels that I burned up because you don't know about it and perhaps it will amuse you. You'd never think so, but they had a ritual that had to be followed if you wanted them to pay attention to your requests. You had to write — by hand and neatly — for example: "Dear angel of health," and ask very succinctly — one supposes that angels have work to do — what you need: "make the analyses come out well ..." Each letter had to finish with: "I'm asking for the good of everyone implicated." Just imagine, of all those implicated ... I couldn't keep myself from rereading the letters before throwing them in the sink and burning them. So much naïveté touched me. How could I be so naïve? I wasn't a child when I wrote those letters! Really, my mind must have started to drift ... In one letter I asked that the cat — I don't remember which cat — stop biting and in another one I wanted the neighbors to stop making noise. I felt miserable, very unhappy, because of the noise. Now it would make me laugh ... Channel 3 or TV 5 as loud as they could make it: how wonderful it would be if I could hear it next year, or the one after ... So much suffering for nothing. Was it Sartre who said that Hell is made up of others? It's not the others, not at all: we ourselves are our Hell. If I could begin my life again I'd be more lighthearted, more carefree, live day by day, like the Epicureans. But I say this and don't believe it. It's normal to take leave burdened by memories, odds and ends, regrets and nostalgia. And everything weighs a lot, especially the remorse for what you've done and the nostalgia for what you've left still to do.

As I was saying: religion has occupied a space in my life and for the moment I prefer its ancient, strict rituals that are more authentic than the phrases from a self-help book of secular ceremonies. Or rather let the priest do what he has to do but he mustn't lay it on too thick: for example, that I had—"I had," he'll say, because I won't be there—a deep faith, because it's not true. When my mother died I prayed a lot. And then nothing: she died. "It's that God can't do everything," they told me. He can't do everything, but, actually, he can do hardly anything and allows a lot of pain and much evil in the world. When I was little, I liked a little boy and would entreat God to make him pay attention to me, to look at me—when I was little, I wasn't very pretty. And he never said a word to me. But I liked praying; the supplications were like a song and if I said them over and over I became drunk from the rhythm and the words, in a kind of ecstasy like what the Sufis experience, very comforting.

Now for the music. Here are the pieces that I'd like everyone to hear. I'm leaving the CDs in the first drawer of the table in my study. I've chosen five of them. I don't know if people will think there are too many. I don't know in what order they should be played. You'll decide.

The first piece is from Scene I, Act II of the opera, *Tito Manlio*. Pure Vivaldi. It's the piece I've heard the most in the last months and it's always consoled, inspired, helped me. The voice is like a pure thread that carries me far away. The aria says: *"Non ti lusinghi la crudeltade / contro d'un core che devi amar. / E per la figlia mostra pietade, / se questo petto vuoi consolar."* It lasts 7.01 minutes but I think that it's worth playing in its entirety because it will give those attending a space for contemplation: they don't have to think about me, but will have a few intimate minutes for themselves, which I'm sure will comfort them.

The second piece is a version of the Adagio of the Concerto BWV 1056 of Bach, adapted and sung by Névoa in Portuguese and titled *Fado Barroco*. It lasts 2.31 minutes. It says: "... *ao tormento / de todo o tempo que nâo estás comigo* ..." It's very beautiful.

The third piece is from the opera *Rinaldo* by Händel, "Lascia ch'io pianga," from the CD, *Farinelli, Il Castrato*. (The two of us went to see the movie by Gérard Corbiau, do you remember? And it affected us deeply.) It lasts 3.59 minutes.

The fourth: the aria "Cantilena," from the *Bachianas Brasileiras*. (It's number 1 on the CD by Heitor Villa-Lobos. A gem.)

The last, may seem frivolous to you: the song "City of Stars," from the movie *La La Land*, sung in a duo by the two lovers. (There's a moment when the girl laughs that I like a lot.) It's a grand story about desires gone wrong, about nostalgia for what could have been and that now can never be. I was in tears in the movie house; they had just given me the diagnosis.

As for the readings, it was more difficult to decide, but finally I picked out a poem by Kavafis translated by Carles Riba* that's entitled, precisely, "Desires," and that speaks of desires that occur without being satisfied. I've marked a place. It's where it says: "Like beautiful bodies of the dead that haven't grown old / and they enclosed them, with tears, inside a splendid tomb ..."

---

* Carles Riba was a Catalan poet, writer, and translator (1893-1959). The Greek poet, Konstantinos Kavafis, lived from 1863 to 1933. (N. of T.)

And to finish, a fragment by John Berger,* from the book, *And Our Faces, My Heart, Brief as Photos*, which is for me the greatest love poem that I've ever read and that speaks of a couple in love, buried side by side, their bones mixed together: "One of your ribs rests on my skull. A metacarpal from my left hand lies inside your pelvis. Like a flower reposing on my perturbed ribs, your breast."

It remains to be seen if you can find someone who reads the texts with some sense of sound and understanding. Be careful especially with the poems. They mustn't be read sing-song; the Berger text has to be rendered with a certain reserve. And, if someone wants to read his or her own work, go ahead! I certainly wouldn't be the one to say no … Ah! the memento.

The memento: be sure that there are enough, because sometimes there aren't enough to go around. Without a cross, a simple card with my name and the following text. Let's see what you think of it. "What knots life makes, and how difficult it is to undo them," by a writer I'm very fond of, and I think it means, precisely, that we ourselves get entangled in a scandalous and useless manner without meaning to.

Looking at the choice I've made, I think that what unites the music and the texts is nostalgia. Earlier I told you: if I were to live my life again, what would I do? If chance permitted me to go backwards

---

* John Berger was an English art critic, novelist, painter and poet (1927-2017). The book title and fragment are in Spanish in the original text. I have replaced them with the original Berger text. (N. of T.)

what would change? What would I do that I haven't done, and that I'd give up doing? Cleaning up I found a photo — I left if for you in the drawer, with the CDs, in case you want to keep it — with you and me, Marta Comas, Anna, Cesc Roure and another boy whose name I couldn't recall. Next to me, as always was S., my first, great, lost love. How many hours you put up with me, listened, consoled me, when I talked to you about him ... When we were together, I was never rid of the fear of losing him, until I finally did lose him. It's a Carnival dinner, we're wearing funny hats and shaggy collars and in the forefront there's a spread of glasses and wine bottles. We're peeing in our pants from all the laughing. I looked at the photo a long time and thought: what has happened to those splendid bodies and tender hearts? And I felt such pain ... Where are we now? Where have we ended up? So many projects ... the entire life to do them ... Everything was a source of enjoyment, even — you're already saying! — our great tragedies, which finally made us laugh. When you're so young you don't know what's in store for you; afterwards life carries you off. You think that you're in command, and you decide so little! But at the time of this photo we were kings, with our grandeur and our little problems ... We were so young! I can assure you that I still remember each kiss, the long afternoons in bed, all the pleasure, everything. And I still ask myself why it couldn't be, what kind of demand, of struggle with myself, of absurd negation, made me think that I didn't have to feel bound to him, if between us there were chains of desire, of hot saliva, of kisses, of sex, of promises and of yearning ... chains like no others that have ever held me, not so many, not so strong, not so gentle. What happened? I still think about it. I don't know if he knows I'm sick. I wouldn't want him to come to see me: he so desired me, those days ... we fit together so well ... as if made for each other ... It was never the same afterwards. When I was young, I'd get very angry with Ignasi — you know all about it — because I found many faults in him. He didn't turn out to be what I wanted. And always S. in my thoughts, an impossible dream. But when all is said and done, Ignasi has been the best man possible to share one's life. He has loved me without fail, tranquilly, absolutely. We've lived together without in any way working hard to do it: in the end, it's about that, an easy life, without having to constantly struggle to decide who is in command, who is the stronger, who needs more, who loves more ... who wins and who loses ... I haven't been absolutely faithful to him ... What he permitted me is what I wouldn't have pardoned him for.

Do you know whom it's such a joy to kiss? Paul's child. He's a child who, as little as he is, looks at things with a bit of sadness. That my son has a son produced a strange sensation in me, and even more when I saw that the boy is like his father, quiet and serious: they bring him and it's as if there weren't a child here. It's curious: Paul's wife talks a blue stream and Alex, her brother, who doesn't stop even under water, lives with a girl who's very reserved. All of us complete each other. But I regret not being able to see the boy grow up. They'll say to him: "Grandma isn't here." They won't tell him that I'm dead, because now it's obvious that you can't say that to children. Perhaps they'll tell him that I've climbed on a star and that I flew up into the sky. The flying Grandma, imagine! Well, let them say what they want. The child is very little and we haven't had the time to weave anything together that will serve him as a memory.

I imagine the people who will be there—few, many? Will they be affected, will they cry, hide their eyes with dark glasses. I'm wondering if S. will come, and if he does, will he find a seat in the first rows or in the last. Thinking about that occupies me. Also, I dream of the possibility—it would please me—that, finally, to honor my person, my two cousins would make peace. At the moment, I don't remember exactly why they quarreled, but I know that it's been more than thirty years that they haven't spoken to each other. The human race … In the end, they'll find a way.

Now it's done. Thank you. You'll do everything very well. Above all, take advantage of each day. They don't come back.